"Let's Play!"

GROUP GAMES
FOR
Preschoolers

Group

Loveland, Colorado

"Let's Play!" Group Games for Preschoolers
Copyright © 1996 Group Publishing, Inc.

Credits
Contributing Authors: Jody Brolsma, Julie Henriksen Bowe, Cindy Dingwall, Ellen Javernick, Barbie Murphy, Lori Haynes Niles, Jennifer Nystrom, Nancy Paulson, Liz Shockey, and Joclyn Wampler
Book Acquisition Editor and Quality Control Editor: Susan L. Lingo
Editors: Beth Rowland Wolf and Jan Kershner
Creative Products Director: Joani Schultz
Copy Editor: Helen Turnbull
Art Director: Helen Lannis
Cover Art Director: Liz Howe
Computer Graphic Artist: Joyce Douglas
Cover Photography: SuperStock, Inc.
Illustrator: Donna Nelson
Production Manager: Ann Marie Gordon

Unless otherwise noted, Scriptures quoted from The Youth Bible, New Century Version, copyright © 1991 by Word Publishing, Dallas, Texas 75039. Used by permission.

Let's play! : group games for preschoolers / {contributing authors, Jody Brolsma, et. al.}.
    p.   cm.
  ISBN 1-55945-613-2
  1. Educational games. 2. Group games. 3. Education, Preschool—Activity programs.
I. Brolsma, Jody.
LB1140.35.E36L48   1996
371.3'97—dc20   96-514
                                       CIP

10 9 8 7 6 5 4 3 2   05 04 03 02 01 00 99 98 97 96
Printed in the United States of America.

Contents

Quiet Times 33

Medium-Energy Games 57

Active Games 79

Songs and Finger Plays 105

►Introduction

Preschoolers' lives are full of wonder, joy, and curiosity. Each day is full of discoveries about the world they live in and the people they know. Preschool children often make those exciting discoveries through play. Play also helps children develop intellect, physical coordination, language, and social skills. And it gives children the chance to try out roles—to pretend being a wiggly caterpillar or a doctor tending patients.

As a preschool leader, you can design playtimes that teach children about God's world. The games in this book will familiarize children with the characters and circumstances of many Bible stories. These games will also help your preschoolers develop caring friendships with each other.

As you plan games for your eager preschoolers, keep these age-level characteristics in mind:

● **Two-year-olds** are naturally focused on themselves. They play alongside each other rather than with each other. Use games in which children play individually in the group as they crawl, roll, walk, jump, or use their arms. Two-year-olds delight in finger plays and action rhymes that use their hands and fingers. Very young children still like to put objects in their mouths, so be sure none of the objects you use presents a choking hazard.

● **Three-year-olds** are beginning to play with friends and are more open to pairs or trios within a game. Help children this age find partners, and reinforce cooperation with hugs and comments such as "I like the way you help each other." Three-year-olds love to hunt for hidden objects or people. They also enjoy games involving large motor-skills such as beanbag tossing or catching bouncy playground balls.

● **Four- and 5-year-olds** are developing more sophisticated friendships. They know that games are more fun when shared with others. Use activities such as simple relays, dramatic play, and passing objects as ways to foster friendships and develop group dynamics.

Enjoy using the noncompetitive, cooperative games in this book. They'll help children feel important, loved, and accepted. Children can play these games confidently and learn about each other and about God's Word as they have loads of fun!

Welcome Games

The Hello Song

Supplies: none

This song will welcome the children to your class and help them learn each other's names.

Let's Play

Have the children sit in a circle. Go around the circle and sing this song until you have welcomed each child by name. Have the children wave to each child they sing to. Sing this song to the tune of "Skip to My Lou."

Hello, (child's name), nice to see you.
Hello, (child's name), nice to see you.
Hello, (child's name), nice to see you.
Welcome to God's church.

To end the game, sing this verse.

God is glad we all are here.
God is glad we all are here.
God is glad we all are here.
We like to come to church.

As you finish the song, have the children jump up, wave their hands, and shout, "Yeah!"

Guess Who?

Supplies: none

This is a fun game to play while learning that God knows everything about us—God even knows how many hairs are on our heads!

10

Let's Play

Form two groups. Have the first group stand facing a wall and the other group quietly stand back to back with the first group. The children facing the wall shouldn't know who's behind them.

Have children in the first group each reach over their shoulders and try to recognize who's behind them by touching that person's head. Give the children in the first group two guesses before they turn around to see who's behind them.

Then switch places. Have the second group of children face the wall while the first group mixes itself up and quietly stands back to back with the second group.

For a fun variation, play this game by hanging poster board from the ceiling so it reaches about six inches above the floor. If you have a large class, have two helpers hold the poster board instead of hanging it from the ceiling. Have the children close their eyes while you tap one child to stand hidden behind the poster board. Invite the rest of the class to identify the child just by looking at his or her shoes.

Play until everyone's had a turn to stand behind the poster board.

It Is Me!

Supplies: blindfold

Children will love the suspense built into this "guess who" game.

Let's Play

Have the children sit in a circle. Choose one child to sit in the middle

and wear a blindfold.

Say this rhyme with the children while you walk around the outside of the circle.

Listen now, and you will hear
The voice of someone who is near.
Can you tell who it might be?

Tap a child on the shoulder, and have him or her complete the rhyme by saying, "It is me!"

The blindfolded child will have two chances to identify the speaker. After two guesses, have the child in the middle take off the blindfold, see who finished the rhyme, and join the circle. Then have the child you tapped sit in the middle to guess the next voice.

Play until everyone has had a chance to sit in the middle of the circle. If your children know each other well, encourage them to disguise their voices.

Flash Dance

Supplies: flashlight

Celebrate your children's talents with this game, and help them understand that their gifts and talents come from God.

Let's Play

Say: **Think of something that you'd like to be or something that you can do well. You might want to be an ice skater or an astronaut. Or maybe you can make a special silly face.**

Give the children a minute to think of a special talent they have or something they'd like to be. Then say: **God gives everyone special gifts, and God wants us to share our gifts with others. Sharing our gifts makes us shine in the world. Let's take turns sharing our gifts.**

Have the children sit in a circle. Then turn off most of the lights. Sing "This Little Light of Mine" with the class, and have the children take

turns making a flashlight beam dance on the walls and ceilings. Caution the children not to hit anyone with the flashlight and not to shine it in anyone's eyes.

After the song, take the flashlight and shine it on each child as he or she acts out a talent. Make up an exciting commentary to go with each child's performance, and include affirmations. For example, if Rhonda acts out ice skating, you might say, "And now in the spotlight is Rhonda, the world's greatest ice skater. Watch as she skates a figure eight. See how she can balance on one leg without falling. Let's give a big hand to Rhonda!" Have the children clap after each performance.

Play until each child has had a turn in the spotlight and has been affirmed.

Path of Praises

Supplies: none

This game will help children practice saying kind things to each other.

Let's Play

Form two lines, and have children stand so each child faces a partner in the opposite line. Have the children stand with space between them so that the lines extend from one end of the room to the other.

Say: **Once when Jesus rode into Jerusalem, everyone praised him and shouted good things about him. We've made a road here between our two lines. Let's say good things about our friends as they walk down this path of praises.**

Have the children raise up their arms and wiggle their hands and fingers. Have the first child in one of the lines walk down the path. As he or she is walking, have the other children yell cheers such as "Hooray!" and "Yeah, (child's name)!"

When the child reaches the end of the road, have him or her rejoin the line. Then have the first child from the other line walk down the path. Continue until everyone has walked down the path of praises.

This game will be even more fun if you let the children blow party horns or play rhythmic instruments to add to their cheers.

Lion's Den

Supplies: none

Use this game with a lesson on Daniel, or any time you want to emphasize the rewards of trusting God.

Let's Play

Have the children stand in a circle. Choose one child to be "Daniel," who will stand in the center of the circle with his eyes closed. Have Daniel, eyes still closed, turn around several times, stop, and point to someone in the circle. Encourage that child to roar and snarl like a lion. Then give Daniel two chances to guess who is the "ferocious lion." For the next round, have the child who roared become the new Daniel. Play until each child has been Daniel.

Make a Friend

Supplies: pairs of socks

This is a great game to use at the beginning of the year to help children meet each other.

Let's Play

Mismatch enough pairs of socks for each child to have one pair. Fold the mismatched socks together, and hand out one pair of socks to each child. Have the children put the socks on their hands.

Then have the children look for someone with the same mismatched pair—one green sock and one red sock, for example.

When the children find their partners, have them trade socks to make a match and then shake hands. If you have time, mismatch the socks, and have the children play again.

►Partner Puzzle

Supplies: scissors, bathroom-tissue tubes, tape, yarn

This game makes getting to know each other fun.

Let's Play

Cut one 20-foot length of yarn for every two children. Use the same color yarn for all of the pieces. Tape each end of each piece of yarn to an empty bathroom-tissue tube. Lay the yarn strings on the floor so they intersect and look like the spokes of a wheel. Use a small piece of yarn to tie a loose knot at the intersection so all yarn strings are wrapped together. Refer to the drawing below.

Have the children stand around the circle and each pick up a bathroom-tissue tube. Have children wrap the yarn around their tubes to discover who is on the other end of their yarn. As the children wrap the yarn around their tubes, their circle will get smaller. When children reach the center of the circle, untie the knot so they can discover who their partners are.

When children have found their partners, have them link elbows and say "hello." Then have the children unwrap the yarn, arrange the circle again, pick up different tubes, and play again.

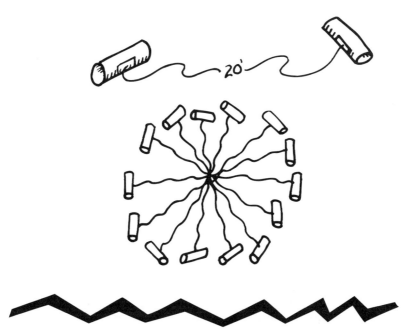

►Wonderfully Made

Supplies: scissors, animal pictures, box with lid

In this fun game, children will discover that they're an important part of God's creation.

Let's Play

Before class, photocopy and cut apart the "Animal Cards" handout, (p. 17), and put the pictures in a box with a lid. Have at least one picture for each child.

Have the children sit in a circle and pass the box around. When you say "stop," have the child holding the box take the top picture out of the box and tell a feature that makes that animal special. For example, a child might say that giraffes are tall or that lions are strong. Then have the child say what makes him or her special. For example, Brad might say that he can run well. Then have Brad say, "Thank you, God, for making (animal name)s, and thank you, God, for making me."

Then have the child put the picture on the floor, replace the lid, and pass the box around the circle again. Repeat this game until everyone has had a chance to choose an animal picture.

►Animal Actions

Supplies: none

Let children develop their dramatic tendencies as they each get a chance in the spotlight.

Animal Cards

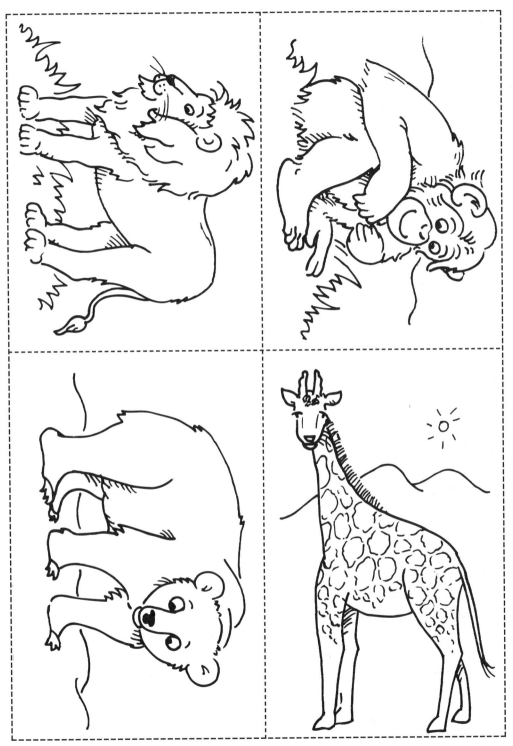

Let's Play

Have the children scatter around the room, and act out this rhyme:

Camels clump *(pat thighs to make hoofbeats),*
Bunnies jump *(jump up),*
Elephants stomp *(stomp in place),*
Ponies romp *(skip in place),*
Tigers prowl *(squint eyes and make stealthy crawling motions with arms),*
Wolves howl *(howl and stretch chin up to the sky),*
But (child's name) can really...

At this point, tap a child on the head and let him or her perform an action such as jumping jacks or twirling around in a circle. Have the rest of the children copy the action. Then repeat the rhyme and tap a different child. Continue until each child has been tapped.

Lost Sheep

Supplies: none

Preschoolers enjoy hiding games, and this one can provide a natural introduction to several Bible stories, including that of the lost sheep in Luke 15.

Let's Play

Choose five or six children to be "sheep." Have them stand in front of the others and bleat like sheep.

Have the other children turn their backs on the sheep or close their eyes. Pick one of the sheep to hide behind an overturned table. Then have the others open their eyes and guess which sheep is missing. The first child to guess correctly switches places with the hidden sheep. Continue until every child has hidden behind the table.

Who Do You Love?

Supplies: none

Children will express love for each other in this fast-paced game and hear how Jesus loves us all.

Let's Play

Have the children sit in a circle. Choose a child to sit in the middle. Have that child point to another child and ask, "Who do you love?"

The child answers by pointing to another child in the circle and saying, "I love (child's name)."

Then the two children sitting in the circle jump up and switch places. Have the children hop to change places. The child in the middle of the circle tries to hop to one of the open places in the circle before the other two children do.

If the child in the middle asks, "Who loves us all?" have the children respond, "Jesus!" Then have everyone jump up and hop around the circle once. Have the children play until everyone has a chance to be in the middle of the circle.

A Friend of Ours

Supplies: none

This is a fun way for children to give each other group hugs.

Let's Play

Play this game in a large room. Have everyone stand in a line shoulder to shoulder and hold hands.

Choose one of the children standing on either end of the line. Say: **Let's sing a song about** (child's name).

"Let's Play!"

Then sing this song to the tune of "London Bridge."

(Child's name) is a friend of ours,
Friend of ours, friend of ours.
(Child's name) is a friend of ours.
We're so glad we know (him or her).

While you sing, have the line twine itself around the child you're singing about. Keep singing until the line has coiled itself into a small circle around the child. Then have the group gently squeeze in tightly to give the child a hug. Keep singing the song while the line unwraps itself back into a straight line.

Have the first child go to the other end of the line, then sing the song to the next child. Continue until the class has sung to every child.

▶Flowers of the Field

Supplies: colored tissue or crepe paper, tape

Children will love dressing themselves as the lovely flowers of the field (Matthew 6:25-34).

Let's Play

Invite children to wrap themselves in colored tissue or crepe paper to look like beautiful flowers in a field. Have tape pieces ready to secure the children's costumes to their clothing.

When everyone has been decorated, have a parade. Then say: **Jesus said that God takes care of flowers by giving them beautiful colored petals to wear. But Jesus also said that God takes care of us even more than he takes care of the flowers. God loves people!**

Have the children rip off their flower costumes so that they once again look like the people God loves. Save the paper scraps to use for craft projects.

Jesus Loves Us

Supplies: none

This game helps children learn each other's names and gives children a chance to show Jesus' love to each other.

Let's Play

Form two groups and have them line up on opposite sides of the room. Have one group pick a child from the opposite group. For example, the group might choose Stephen. Then have the children call out, "Jesus loves us; this we know. Send Stephen over, and we'll tell him so."

Have Stephen hop over to the group that called him. Have the children surround him with a group hug and say, "Jesus loves you, Stephen."

Then let the other group choose a child to come over for a hug. Continue the game until everyone has been shown Jesus' love.

Pass the Names

Supplies: markers, index cards

Use this game to help children recognize their names in writing and to give them a fun way to socialize.

Let's Play

Write each child's name on an index card. Give each child his or her card and spell the name aloud while you point to the letters. Older children can write their own names on the cards.

Have the children sit in a circle. On "go," have them pass the name cards around the circle as quickly as they can. When you call out "change," have them change directions. Call out "change" several times. Then call out "find" and have the children scramble to find their own name cards.

Go around the circle and have each child say his or her name and point to the letters while spelling the name out loud.

If you're playing with younger children, add an identifying shape such as a star or heart to each child's card for easy identification.

►A Breezy Good Time

Supplies: markers, old bedsheet, cassette player, tape of praise music

Bring a simple prop from home and watch children enjoy being in the middle of this breezy game.

Let's Play

Draw a happy face near the edge of a sheet or on an old, round tablecloth. Have the children stand around the bedsheet and hold it waisthigh with both hands. Play praise music and have the children pass the sheet around the circle. When the music stops, whoever is closest to the happy face sits underneath the sheet in the middle of the circle.

The other children gently raise and lower the sheet so the child underneath is treated to a gentle breeze. While the children are raising and lowering the sheet, have them say, "Here's a soft and gentle breeze. Just for you, it's sure to please." Then the child rejoins the circle. Play until everyone has had a chance to enjoy the gentle breeze.

Mail

Supplies: index cards, envelopes, crayons or pencils

Here's a game that will allow children to playact as they learn to recognize letters and names. This activity really "delivers"!

Let's Play

Have the children sit in a circle. Give each child an index card, an envelope, and a crayon or pencil. Have the children write their names or draw pictures on the cards and envelopes. Make sure the same name or picture is on both the envelope and card.

Tell the children to keep the cards but to put the envelopes in a pile in the middle of the circle. Mix up the envelopes. Choose one child to draw an envelope from the pile and "deliver the mail" to the owner by matching the name or picture on the envelope with that on the index card. Help the child read the name on the envelope and the name on the card. Then have the child return to his or her place in the circle. Have the child whose envelope was drawn choose and deliver the next envelope.

Play until all the mail has been delivered.

Make a Match

Supplies: pairs of related items, such as socks and shoes, pencils and paper, or a flower and vase

This game will help children develop sequential thinking skills as they enjoy a unique getting-to-know-you activity.

Let's Play

Gather pairs of related items, such as shoes and socks, pencil and paper, a vase and flower, and a brush and comb. It's OK to repeat pairs

23

of items. Give each child one of the items. Then have the children wander around the room until they find the person whose item goes with their own. When children make their matches, have them sit down with their partners. When all the children are sitting, have each pair stand, introduce each other, and show their matching pair of items.

Gather all of the items, redistribute them and have the children play again.

 I See

Supplies: none

This fun version of I Spy sharpens children's observations and allows younger and older children to interact.

Let's Play

Have the children sit in a circle. Secretly choose one child, and say: **I see someone who's wearing…** Complete the sentence by naming something that child is wearing, such as glasses, a hair bow, or a blue shirt. Then have the children guess who you see.

If the children can't guess, give them another clue about the person you've chosen. Your clue might be about something the child likes to do, what color his or her eyes are, what kind of pets the child has, or how many brothers and sisters the child has. When the children guess who you've chosen, secretly choose another child, and play again.

Young preschoolers will have fun just guessing who you've chosen. Older preschoolers will enjoy giving the clues about someone they've chosen. Play until each child has been chosen.

Kindness Leis

Supplies: ½ × 6-inch paper strips in bright colors, glue stick

Here's a game and a craft in one! Take-home leis will remind children of the kind comments they received in class.

Let's Play

Have the children sit in a circle. Choose one child to sit in the middle. Have another child take a paper strip and say something kind to the child in the center, such as "I have fun when I play with you" or "You're my friend."

Then have the child with the paper strip make a loop and glue it with the glue stick. Have the next child say something kind to the child in the middle of the circle and thread a paper strip through the looped strip and glue it.

Continue until every child has said something kind to the child in the middle of the circle, and has added a paper strip to the chain. Then use one more paper strip to join the ends of the chain together to form a lei. (If necessary, add more loops to the chain to make it long enough to go over the child's head.) Put the lei over the child's head and say: **Always remember that you're special to our class.**

Choose another child to sit in the middle of the circle. Continue until everyone has a "kindness lei" to wear home.

Come Aboard

Supplies: masking tape

Use this affirmation to call children from individual play to group activities.

25

Let's Play

Create a boat shape with masking tape on the floor. Make sure the boat is big enough for all the children to fit inside. One by one call the children to leave their play areas and come aboard your boat. Use this poem to call the children or sing the rhyme to the tune of "London Bridge."

(Child's name), (Child's name), leave your play.
Come aboard right away.
On our boat we'll cross the sea.
Come along and sail with me.

You may need to repeat the poem to get a child's attention. As children join you in the boat, tell them why you're glad they've joined you. You might say you're glad Jim is with you because he's a careful listener. You might tell Michelle that she is a good helper. Have the children in the boat say the rhyme with you to call the next child until everyone comes aboard.

►Shining Stars

Supplies: drawing of a five-pointed star

Each child in your class is a star. Bring home the point of Philippians 2:15 with this affirmation.

Let's Play

Have the children stand with their legs and arms spread wide. Show them the picture of the star, and say: **Look how your body makes a star!**

Count the five points of each child's body that make a star: two feet, two hands, and a head. Encourage the children to count with you.

Say: **The Bible says that we shine like stars in a dark world. Let's shine like stars now.**

Have the children walk around the room, waving their arms and wiggling their fingers like "twinkling stars."

Then mention why each child shines like a star. You might tell Tiffany that she is always kind, or you might tell Brent that you like the way he shares his toys.

Then have the children twinkle at each other while you sing "Twinkle, Twinkle, Little Star."

►Silly Pets

Supplies: none

Promote cooperation in this game for older preschoolers.

Let's Play

Encourage children to think of unusual animals to use as pets. Have the children form pairs for this silly game. In their pairs, have the children decide who will be the first pet and what kind of pet to be. For example, Jamie and Alex may decide that Alex will be the pet and that Alex wants to be a seal. Have Alex and Jamie come up with a trick that a pet seal might do, such as clapping its hands or balancing a ball on its nose.

When all of the pairs know what they'll do, gather the group together. Have children introduce their pets by saying, "This is my pet (animal) and this is its special trick." Then have the pets pretend to do their tricks.

When everyone has introduced his or her pet, have the partners switch roles and play again, choosing different animals.

►The Name Song

Supplies: none

Your children will shine when they hear their names in this song.

27

Let's Play

Have the children sit in a circle. Sing the song "Twinkle, Twinkle, Little Star," replacing all of the words with the children's names. Go in order around the circle, fitting in the names as best you can. Continue singing until you've included all the children in the circle. Your song might go something like this:

Rebecca, Samson, Donny, Joe,
Suzy, Fred, and Amanda.
Mary Jane, Ashley, Pete,
Jonathan, and Elizabeth.
Anna, Kyle, and then there's Zoe,
Jennifer, Hannah, and Marie.

If you run out of names before the end of the song, you can either continue around the circle until the verse is over, or you can simply end the song. Don't worry about getting the tune perfect. The children will enjoy singing their names even if the names don't quite fit the tune.

The first time around the circle, have the children each wave their hands or star-shaped cookies as you sing their names. The second time around, have all of the children point to the child whose name you're singing.

Water From the Well

Supplies: brown poster board, tape, bowl, apple juice, scissors, paper cups
This game introduces children to the idea of serving each other and encourages them to follow Jesus' example.

Let's Play

Put a big bowl filled with juice on a low table. Make the bowl look like a well by taping a piece of brown poster board in a wide tube around it. Cut a strip of poster board, and arch it over the top to look like the

top of the well. See the drawing below. Put a stack of paper cups by the well. Have the children line up on the opposite side of the room.

Say: **Jesus said we could show our love for him by serving each other. Let's show our love for Jesus by serving each other a cool drink right now.**

Stand by the well. Have the first child in line walk over to the well. Using a paper cup as a dipper, dip a small amount of juice into a paper cup, and give it to the child. Have the class say: **We love Jesus, and we love you, too.** After the child drinks the juice, help him or her take a fresh cup and dip a small amount of juice for the next child in line.

Continue until everyone has been affirmed and served a refreshing drink.

The Prodigal Children

Supplies: none

In this game, children act out a favorite Bible story from Luke 15:11-32.

Let's Play

Form two groups, the "parents" and the "children." Have the parents stand on one side of the room and the children stand on the other side. On "go" have the children say, "I'm coming home, Mom (or Dad)." Have the parents respond, "We're glad because we've missed you."

Then have the children and the parents all hop to the middle of the room. Each parent pairs up with a child by linking arms, then they skip or walk around in circles. Signal the pairs to stop with a whistle or a

29

clap, and have parents and children return to opposite sides of the room.

Have children switch roles and play again.

Jesus Loves You

Supplies: none

Share Jesus' love with each child in this game.

Let's Play

Form a circle and choose a child to stand in the middle. Have the children hold hands as you sing this song with them to the tune of "Clementine," or repeat the words as a poem. As you sing the first two lines, have the group walk into the center of the circle until they've formed a tight group around the child in the middle. As you sing the last two lines, have the children back up.

Jesus loves you. Jesus loves you. *(Walk to the center.)*
Jesus loves you as you are. *(Walk to the center.)*
You're a special friend to Jesus. *(Return to the circle.)*
Jesus loves you as you are. *(Return to the circle.)*

Then choose another child to stand in the middle. Continue until you've sung to every child.

Children of God

Supplies: none

Use this action game to help the children realize they're children of God.

Let's Play

Have the children scatter around the room. Encourage children to follow the motions in this action game.

Children of God, wave your hands.
Children of God, jump up and down.
Children of God, turn around.
Children of God, reach for the sky.
Children of God, hop on one foot.
Children of God, hug a friend.
Children of God, sit on the ground.
Children of God, giggle and laugh.
Children of God, let's say "amen."

To play again, have the children suggest actions for the children of God to do.

►The Goodbye Song

Supplies: none

This affirming song will help children remember good things about your class as they leave each week.

Let's Play

Sing this song to the tune of "Looby Loo." Continue repeating the second verse until you've mentioned each child by name.

This is the end of class.
We've had a lot of fun.
We'll say goodbye until next time.
Dippity, doopity, dum.

"Let's Play!"

We say goodbye to (child's name).
To (child's name), (child's name), and (child's name).
We'll say goodbye until next time.
Dippity, doopity, dum.

   Squeeze each child's hand gently, or pat each child on the shoulder as they leave your classroom.

Quiet Times

Tangrams

Supplies: scissors, construction paper

Spark creativity and help children learn basic shapes as they form geometric figures in this fun game.

Let's Play

Cut circles, squares, rectangles, and triangles from construction paper in different colors. You can use giant confetti for this game, too.

Give each child a handful of shapes. Have the children arrange their shapes to create pictures. For example, you might have the children make trees, dogs, flowers, or people. Have the children "erase" their pictures by scattering the shapes. Encourage the children to share shapes and colors while they create.

You can also use this game to encourage children to create pictures from your lesson's Bible story.

The Rename Game

Supplies: unsharpened pencil

Adam gave the animals their names originally, but your children will have fun renaming them.

Let's Play

Have the children sit in a circle on the floor. Use an unsharpened pencil as a pointer, and show the children how to spin it.

Have a child spin the pointer. When the pencil stops spinning, have the child to whom it's pointing name an animal, such as a kangaroo. Then have that child spin the pointer. When it stops spinning, have the child to whom it's pointing name a second animal, such as a cat.

Combine the two animals into a brand-new animal, and have all the children show how that animal would move and sound. For example, a "kangaroo-cat" might jump like a kangaroo and meow or purr like a cat. In this game, silly is best. Your kids might create "bunny-dogs," "elephant-mice," or "whale-birds."

Play until everyone has contributed to an animal name.

►Believers' Belongings

Supplies: small toys, cassette player, tape of praise music

Strengthen the sharing skills of your young preschoolers with this game of friendly fun.

Let's Play

Have the children sit in a circle. Say: **The people in the very first church shared what they had with each other. We can share too! Friends share their toys, their food, and their fun. Let's have fun right now with this sharing game.**

Give each child a small toy from the room. Play praise music, and have the children pass the toys around the circle all at once. Stop the music periodically. When the music stops, have the children all say, "Thank you for sharing the (name of toy they're holding)."

Continue playing as long as time allows. For added fun, have the children pass the toys in opposite directions with their eyes closed or as quickly as possible.

Let Your Fingers Do the Talking

Supplies: none

If your preschoolers are wound up, calm them down with this quiet game.

Let's Play

Tell the children that their lips have been buttoned shut, but they can still communicate by using their hands.

Have the children say the following words or phrases using just their hands.

- Hello! *(wave)*
- Great job! *(high five or thumbs up)*
- Stop! *(hand up, palm facing front)*
- Come here! *(beckon with a single finger)*
- Quiet! *(finger in front of lips)*
- Goodbye! *(wave)*

You can also have the children quietly imitate animals such as bunnies or kittens. You might even try singing a favorite action song without the words.

You'll be amazed at how quiet your class can be!

Shoe Capers

Supplies: none

Two- and 3-year-olds love the simple concept of this game. Use it as an icebreaker with older children.

36

Let's Play

Have each child take off one shoe and put it in a pile on the floor. Have the children sit in a circle around the pile of shoes.

Let each child take a turn pulling a shoe from the pile and asking, "Yoo-hoo! Whose shoe?"

The owner will call out, "My shoe! My shoe!" and take the shoe. Play until everyone has retrieved his or her shoe.

Older preschoolers will enjoy walking around the room with someone else's shoe while searching for their own shoes.

Joyful Noises

Supplies: none

Making a joyful noise to the Lord never sounded quite like this!

Let's Play

Sit in a circle on the floor. Say: **Let's make a joyful noise to God!**

Make a funny sound, and have the person on your left make the same sound. Keep going around the circle until everyone's made that sound.

Then have the person on your left make a different funny sound, and have everyone around the circle make that sound. See how fast the sound can make it around the circle.

Play until everyone has chosen a joyful sound to spread around the circle. For older preschoolers, use phrases instead of sounds, or spread "joyful actions" such as clapping, hopping, or waving.

What God Has Made

Supplies: none

This is a good outdoor game.

Let's Play

Sit in a circle with the children. Begin by saying: **I see something God has made. It's white and fluffy, and it's way up high. What do I see?**

The children will answer, "a cloud." Play until children understand the game. Then have them take turns describing and guessing other things that God has made.

Vary the difficulty of this game by offering more hints or fewer hints. End this game by inviting children to draw pictures of things they identified during the game.

God Gave Me A...

Supplies: none

This is a silly game that will have your children giggling in no time!

Let's Play

Have the children sit in a circle. Have one child choose a feature that everyone has, such as a nose.

Have the child say to the group, "God gave me a nose." But the child will point to another feature, such as a foot.

The rest of the children will respond, "A what?"

The first child will say, "A nose" and will point to his or her foot.

The group will answer, "Oh! God gave you a nose." Then the children will tap their noses.

The next child will choose another feature, such as hair, and say, "God gave me hair," but he or she may point to a knee.

The key is for the children to listen carefully and not be distracted by the visual clues. Once the children understand this game, they'll giggle at calling their eyes "toes" and their mouths "bellybuttons." This game becomes more fun as the children call out features more quickly.

Going to Jerusalem

Supplies: none

Kids love to take pretend journeys. Travel back to Jerusalem with this imaginative game.

Let's Play

Say: **When Jesus was growing up, many people didn't get to go to the Temple every week to worship God. The Temple was far away, so they only went for very special occasions. The journey to the Temple in Jerusalem was a long and special trip. Let's play a game about going to Jerusalem.**

Have the children pretend to pack their bags as they say this verse with you:

I'm going to Jerusalem.
I know that I'll have fun.
I'm going to Jerusalem;
I'll take along some . . .

Have the child on your right suggest something that might be good to take on a trip, such as toothpaste, pajamas, or snacks.

Then repeat the verse together, and have the next child contribute an idea. When everyone has offered a suggestion, end the game with this verse:

I'm going to Jerusalem.
I know that I'll have fun.
I'm going to Jerusalem;
Now our trip is done.

For more fun, pass a small backpack or suitcase around your group as you play. When you finish each verse, have the child holding the backpack suggest an item to take on the journey.

Mirror Imitation

Supplies: none

This game is especially suited to lessons about imitating or following God.

Let's Play

Have the children sit so they're facing you. Have them imitate your actions as you recite this poem:

I look in the mirror, and what do I see? *(Cup hands next to eyes.)*
I see a happy face smiling at me. *(Smile broadly.)*
I look in the mirror, and what do I see? *(Cup hands next to eyes.)*
I see fingers waving at me. *(Wave fingers.)*
I look in the mirror, and what do I see? *(Cup hands next to eyes.)*
I see a sleepy head nodding at me. *(Pretend to sleep.)*
I look in the mirror, and what do I see? *(Cup hands next to eyes.)*
I see hands clapping for me. *(Clap hands.)*
I look in the mirror, and what do I see? *(Cup hands next to eyes.)*
I see an eye winking at me. *(Wink eye.)*

Older preschoolers will enjoy taking turns coming up with actions for the class to imitate. Let several children contribute additional verses and actions to the poem.

For more fun, have the children make mirrors by covering paper plates with aluminum foil. You may also want to bring a hand mirror to play with before or after the game.

Bumper Balls

Supplies: variety of balls such as Ping-Pong balls, tennis balls, racquet-balls, baseballs, playground balls, and soccer balls

Even young preschoolers will like this bouncy action game.

Let's Play

You'll need some kind of ball for each child. Use balls of many different sizes and materials.

Have all the children sit cross-legged in a tight circle so that everyone's knees are touching. Give each child a ball. Have the children roll their balls across the circle at the same time, then scramble to get one of the balls that comes their way.

When everyone's retrieved a ball, start the game again.

Circle Ball

Supplies: playground ball, piece of paper

Children who are learning to count will enjoy this game.

Let's Play

Have the children sit in a circle. Give one child a ball. Put a piece of paper in front of that child to remind everyone where the ball starts in the circle.

Call out a number, such as five, and have the children pass the ball around the circle that many times. When the ball has gone all the way around the circle one time, have the group call out, "One!" Have them call out the number each time the ball makes a trip around the circle. When the children have passed around the ball the designated number of times, have them yell, "Hooray!" and wave their hands.

"Let's Play!"

Begin the game again by handing the "starting paper" to another child, then call out a new number.

Older preschoolers will enjoy seeing how fast they can pass the ball around the circle.

Sand Search

Supplies: sandbox or dishpan full of clean sand; spoons, shovels, and kitchen strainers; small objects such as erasers or small toys. (Make sure none of the objects you choose poses a swallowing danger.)

Children love the feel of sand running through their fingers. Combine sensory stimulation with the anticipation of finding hidden "treasure."

Let's Play

In a sandbox filled with clean sand, bury at least three erasers or small toys for every child.

Provide spoons, shovels, and kitchen strainers, and let the children sift through the sand for the hidden treasures. Play until the children find all the items. Then let children count their items aloud. Bury the treasures and play again. Make sure each child finds a hidden item.

If you don't have a sandbox, try hiding photocopies of coins in a cardboard box full of shredded paper.

Caterpillar Crawl

Supplies: old bedsheet

Children will love pretending to be a long, creepy-crawly caterpillar in this game.

42

Let's Play

Tie knots in both ends of an old bedsheet. Lay the sheet on the floor at one end of the room, and have the children kneel in a line under the sheet. Make sure the child at the "head" of the caterpillar can peek out from under the sheet.

Have the children shuffle on their knees like a giant caterpillar. Sing this song to the tune of "I'm a Little Teapot" while your crawly caterpillar creeps in a circle around the room:

I'm a caterpillar;
See me crawl.
I'll grow long
But not too tall.
I can keep a-crawling all day long
As I sing this happy song.

If you have time and the weather's nice, take a trip outside to search for real caterpillars.

Carry a Friend

Supplies: towel, balloon

This is a good game to play when you're teaching the story about the paralyzed man who was lowered through a roof to Jesus (Mark 2:1-12).

Let's Play

Form two groups, and have each group line up shoulder to shoulder

and face the other group no more than four feet apart. Tell every other child in each group to kneel.

Have the first two children facing each other hold a towel stretched out between them. Put a balloon on the towel to represent the paralyzed man. Have the children pass the towel to the kneeling children beside them. Then have the kneeling children pass the towel up to the next children, who are standing beside them. Have the children continue passing the towel and balloon to the end of the line. If the balloon falls off the towel, just have the children replace it.

Then have the standing children kneel and the kneeling children stand to play the game again.

Softly Search

Supplies: clock with an audible ticking sound or battery-powered radio

Use this game as a natural introduction to quiet time in your class.

Let's Play

Hide the clock or radio before the children arrive or while they're in another room. Have the children sit silently and listen for the ticking sound. Then have them search for the clock without talking or making any noises. Once the children find the clock, have them give a silent cheer.

To play another round, have the child who found the clock hide it for the other children to find.

Wahoo!

Supplies: markers, index cards or scraps of paper, or game cards from Candyland

This game helps children learn their colors while they're having fun.

Let's Play

Use the cards from a Candyland game, or make your own cards by drawing different-colored shapes on index cards or scraps of paper. Make about 10 cards for each child. If you have more than six children, form two groups. Each group will need a teen or adult helper.

Have the children sit in a tight circle. Give each child the same number of cards. Have the children place their cards face down in a pile in front of them. Call out a color, such as red. Have children go around the circle and take turns turning over one card at a time and putting it in a pile in the middle of the circle. Whenever a red card is turned over, have the children all shout, "Wahoo!" and shake their hands in the air. Then gather the cards from the middle and put them aside.

When the children have played all their cards, shuffle the deck and re-deal the cards. Call out another color to start the game again.

You can also use this game to teach children shapes by creating a set of cards with different geometric shapes on them.

►The Lost Coin

Supplies: cardboard, marker, scissors

Introduce this game when your lesson is about the woman who lost her coin (Luke 15:8-10).

Let's Play

Make a "coin" by cutting out a small circle from cardboard and drawing on it the features from a real coin, such as "25 cents" or "In God We Trust."

Have the children sit in a circle. Choose one child to be the "woman" who lost the coin. Have the woman sit in the middle and close her eyes while the other children pass the coin around the circle. When the woman says, "I have lost my coin," have the children stop passing the coin. All of the children will make fists, including the child who has the coin. When the woman opens her eyes, she has two guesses to find the player who has the coin. If the woman guesses correctly, she trades places with the child who has the coin. If the woman guesses incorrectly, she stays in the middle for another round.

For extra fun, pass a round cracker as the coin. Provide fresh snack-cracker "coins" to munch after playing.

▶ The Quiet Train

Supplies: none

Use this game to make a smooth transition from noisy activities to more quiet ones.

Let's Play

Put your finger to your lips, and whisper: **Shh, shh, shh, shh.** Quietly walk around the room, and tap children on the shoulders as you continue to whisper: **Shh, shh, shh, shh.**

As the children are tapped, have them join in line behind you, put their fingers to their lips, and whisper with you. As you travel around the room, you'll soon sound like a very quiet train.

When all the children are in line behind you, lead them around the room once, then have them sit in the area you've prepared for the next activity.

Shape Play

Supplies: none

This large-motor-skills game helps get the wiggles out as it teaches children different shapes.

Let's Play

Ask: **What kinds of shapes has God made?**

For each shape the children mention, have them lie on the floor and together form that shape with their bodies. Be sure to use every child, no matter what shape the class is making. Children might choose to make squares, rectangles, circles, or triangles.

When the children can't think of any more shapes to make, say: **God made unusual shapes, too! Let's make an unusual shape.** Have children make a squiggly shape with many bends, curves, and angles.

Loop-the-Loop Races

Supplies: cereal loops, cardboard wrapping-paper tubes, large plastic bowl

This game works well with a lesson about the poor widow who gave all she had (Luke 21:1-4).

Let's Play

Place chairs in a tight circle with the backs of the chairs facing inward. Place a large bowl in the middle of the circle. Give each child 10 cereal loops and a wrapping-paper tube. If you don't have wrapping-paper tubes, make tubes by rolling up large sheets of newspaper and taping them. Show the children how to hold their tubes so they rest on the tops of the chair backs.

Put a cereal loop inside the tube, and tilt the tube up so the loop rolls down and falls into the bowl. Have the children see how many of their cereal loops fall into the bowl.

When the class has finished playing, save the "old" cereal for the birds to enjoy, then give each child a handful of fresh cereal to munch.

How Do I Feel?

Supplies: none

Help older children identify feelings with this activity.

Let's Play

Have the children sit in a circle on the floor. Pause after you read each of the following statements to allow children time to respond.

- **Show me what your face would look like if you were angry.**
- **Show me what your face would look like if you were happy.**
- **Show me what your face would look like if you were sad.**
- **Show me what your face would look like if you were sleepy.**

Say: **Now I'm going to read some other sentences. Decide how you would feel if the situation happened to you, then look at the person across the circle from you and make a face to show how you'd feel.**

Read each of the following situations aloud to the children. Pause after each statement so children can make faces that show how they'd feel. Expect to hear a few giggles when the children make angry and sad faces at each other.

- **You drop your ice cream cone.**
- **It's Christmas morning, and it's time to open presents.**
- **You fall down and skin your knee.**
- **Your friend won't give you a toy you want to play with.**

- **It's very late at night, and you are so tired.**
- **You just got permission to play with your best friend.**

As a variation, allow children to take turns telling their own situations to the class.

Sowing Seeds

Supplies: Poster board or cardboard, plastic bowl, scissors, markers, cereal loops or raisins, pencil

Older preschoolers will enjoy playing this game after hearing Jesus' parable of the sower (Matthew 13:1-23).

Let's Play

Make a game spinner by cutting a 5×5-inch square from poster board or cardboard. Trim the corners to create an octagon. Draw lines from the center of the octagon to each corner to create eight sections. In each section, draw or write one of the following: a bird; rocks; weeds; and the numbers 1, 2, 3, 4, and 5. Insert a pencil through the center of the octagon to create a spinning top. See the picture below.

Give each child 10 cereal loops or raisins for "seeds." Place a bowl in the center of the group. Say: **Let's pretend this bowl is our garden. We'll take turns planting our pretend seeds.**

Let each child take a turn spinning the top. If the pencil lands on a number, he or she must "plant" that number of seeds in the garden. If the pencil lands on the bird, rocks, or weeds, the child must take one seed from the garden and add it to his or her own pile of seeds.

Have the children play for as long as they like or until all the seeds are planted.

Who Scratched?

Supplies: small toy or eraser

This is a fun, quiet, listening game that kids will want to play again and again.

Let's Play

Arrange one chair for each child around a table. Have the children each stand behind one of the chairs, holding their cupped hands behind their backs. Walk around the circle, and put a small toy or eraser in one child's hand. Make sure the object you choose does not pose a swallowing danger. As you walk around the circle, pretend to put the toy in each child's hand. When you get all the way around the circle, have the children sit in the chairs with their hands underneath the table and their heads down with one ear against the table top.

Tell whoever has the toy to lightly scratch the underside of the table. Then have the children lift up their heads and guess who has the toy. When the children have guessed correctly, have them take their places behind the chairs to play again.

Shape Bingo

Supplies: paper, markers, cereal loops, index cards

This simplified Bingo game is great fun for children who are learning shapes and colors.

Let's Play

On a sheet of paper, draw a grid with nine squares. Photocopy enough sheets for each child to have one. Then fill in the grid boxes with shapes in different colors, using three shapes and three colors. Use the diagram

50

below as an example. On each grid, put the shapes in different places so that none of the grids is exactly like another.

Then draw the same shapes in the same colors on nine index cards. Be sure each grid box is represented by a shape and color. For example, if you have a blue triangle in one grid box, be sure to draw a blue triangle on an index card.

Give each child one of the grids and a handful of cereal loops.

Shuffle the index cards. Draw a card, and call out the shape and the color—a blue triangle or a yellow square, for example.

Have the children put a cereal loop on the correct color and shape. For children who are just learning shapes and colors, show them the card. Continue drawing cards until the children have filled their entire cards with cereal loops. The first child to fill an entire card with cereal loops can shout, "Jesus loves me!" to end the game.

As children become familiar with the shapes, add variations of traditional Bingo games, such as filling diagonal spaces, or corners. You can also play this game by using letters of the alphabet instead of shapes or colors.

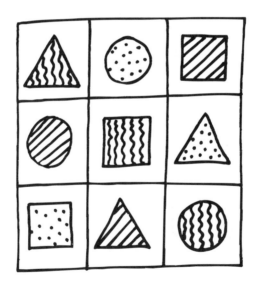

Story Pictures

Supplies: sandpaper sheets, yarn in 6-inch and 12-inch pieces

The budding artists in your class will enjoy this unusual way to illustrate any story. The best part for you? No messy cleanup!

Let's Play

Give each child a sheet of coarse sandpaper and several lengths of different-colored yarn.

As you tell the children a Bible story, have the children "draw" pictures of the story by arranging the yarn on the sandpaper—the yarn will stick to the sandpaper as it would on flannel board!

Have the children show their pictures to each other. Then have them erase the pictures by pulling off the yarn.

You can also use this activity as a getting-to-know-you game by having the children create pictures of their families or favorite toys, places, and favorite foods.

Collect the supplies after each use, and keep them handy on your shelf for a quick addition to stories or play.

Jacob and Esau

Supplies: pair of clean socks

This game is just right for older children when you're studying the story of Jacob and Esau (Genesis 27–28).

Let's Play

Have children play this game in trios. Choose one child to be "Isaac." Choose two others to be "Jacob" and "Esau." Give Jacob and Esau each

52

a sock to put on one hand.

Have Isaac close his eyes. Tell Jacob and Esau to decide secretly who will hold Isaac's hand. Have the one who is chosen hold Isaac's hand with a sock-covered hand. Give Isaac one chance to guess who is holding his hand.

Have the children play several rounds and trade places each round.

Circle Drawings

Supplies: none

This ticklish game feels great and serves as a fun icebreaker.

Let's Play

Have the children sit cross-legged in a circle facing right so that they're looking at the back of the child next to them.

Have the children use their fingers to draw pictures on the backs of the children in front of them while you tell this story. Say: **One day, Robert and Roberta went outside to play. Draw Robert and Roberta.** *Pause.* **The sun was shining brightly. Draw the sun.** *Pause.* **They took their dog Bitsey to the park with them. Draw Bitsey.** *Pause.*

On the way to the park they saw flowers. Draw the flowers. *Pause.* **And they saw trees. Draw the trees.** *Pause.* **When they arrived at the park they played ball with Bitsey. They threw the ball. Use one finger to draw which way the ball went.** *Pause.* **And Bitsey would catch the ball in her teeth and trot back with it. Use two fingers to show Bitsey running back with the ball.** *Pause.*

Soon a cloud came over the sun. Draw a cloud. *Pause.* **And the wind began to blow. Blow on your friend's back.** *Pause.* **Then the rain came down. Lightly tap out raindrops with your fingers.** *Pause.* **And Robert, Roberta, and Bitsey ran all the way home. Run your fingers up your friend's back.** *Pause.*

To end the game, have the children give each other a quick back rub or gentle scratch.

Echo Rhythms

Supplies: none

Use this game to help children follow simple rhythms.

Let's Play

Have the children sit cross-legged on the floor where they can see you. Come up with a short rhythm that they can clap. For example, you might clap the rhythmic syllables of the words "lightly row, lightly row"—two short claps followed by a long clap, then repeat.

Say the following three words to the children in a rhythmic pattern with accents on "now" and on the first syllable of "listen." Say: **Now you listen.** And immediately clap the rhythm.

Then say to the children: **Now you clap.** And have them immediately echo your clapping rhythm.

Keep practicing until you can complete the entire sequence without missing a beat. Then go on to another rhythm. Consider clapping these words:

- Mis-sis-sip-pi Ri-ver—short, short, short, short, long, long
- Heav-en-ly Heav-en-ly—triplet, triplet
- Heav-en-ly Sun-light—triplet, long, long
- This Lit-tle Light of Mine—long, short, short, long, long, long

It may help children remember the rhythm if you say the words aloud as you're clapping them.

Over, Under, Through

Supplies: stuffed animals or puppets

Combine following directions with motor-skill coordination in this fun song.

Let's Play

Each child will need a small stuffed animal or puppet for this game. If you don't have enough stuffed animals, use pairs of socks rolled into balls.

Tell the children to sit on the floor with their knees bent and their feet flat on the floor. Have the children begin the game by setting the stuffed animal on their knees. Sing this song to the tune of "The Mulberry Bush" and show the children how to act out the motions with the stuffed animals.

Verse 1: *(Pass the animal under your knees each time you sing "through the gate.")*

The animals went through the gate,
Through the gate, through the gate.
The animals went through the gate
All day long.

Verse 2: *(Pass the animal over your knees each time you sing "over the gate.")*

The animals went over the gate,
Over the gate, over the gate.
The animals went over the gate
All day long.

Verse 3: *(Pass the animal around your ankles each time you sing "around the gate.")*

The animals went around the gate,
Around the gate, around the gate.
The animals went around the gate
All day long.

For extra fun, host a tea party for the children and their stuffed animals after the game.

Who Am I?

Supplies: poster board, glue sticks, scissors, animal pictures

This is an easy way to simplify the game Twenty Questions for young children.

Let's Play

Take pages from old coloring books or picture books that show one item on a page. Used coloring books of animals are great for this game.

Glue the pages to individual sheets of poster board. Then cut eye-holes in the sheets of poster board so the children can hold the pictures up to their faces as masks.

Put the poster board masks face down. Choose a child to be "It." Have It pick up the first mask and hold it to his or her eyes without looking at the picture on the mask. Have the other children describe the picture on the mask. For example, if the picture is a lion, one child might say, "You live in the jungle." Another child might say, "You growl." Someone else might say, "You have a mane." Younger children may enjoy giving "sound clues" for each animal. Have the children give clues until It guesses the picture.

Then choose another child to be It. Continue the game until each child has had a chance to be It.

Medium–Energy Games

Blankets

Supplies: felt, permanent marker, scissors, masking tape, blindfold

Play this version of Pin the Tail on the Donkey when your class is learning about baby Moses, baby Samuel, or baby Jesus.

Let's Play

Attach a large square of felt to a wall. Use a permanent marker to draw a baby on the felt, or cut out a baby pattern from felt and attach it to the felt square. Give each child a piece of felt to cover the baby like a blanket. Attach a piece of masking tape to the edge of each felt piece.

Blindfold the children one at a time and have them try to cover the baby with their blankets. The other children may offer directions to help the blindfolded child find and cover the baby.

Jesus Calms the Sea

Supplies: none

Play this imaginative game when you're studying the story of Jesus calming the sea (Mark 4:35-41).

Let's Play

Have the children stand in a circle with plenty of room between them. Say: **Today we'll pretend to be a stormy sea. Listen closely and follow my actions.**

The sea was calm at first. Stand with your arms out to your sides.

Gentle waves rocked the boat that Jesus and the disciples were sailing in. Sway back and forth like gentle waves.

Then a storm blew in, and the waves got bigger. Sway faster, and wave your arms in a hula fashion.

The waves got bigger and stronger—the sea was splashing wildly! Sway even faster, and wave your arms in a bigger pattern.

Then Jesus said, "Be still!" Drop to the floor.

And the stormy sea was silent! Put your finger to your lips.

Play again and see how quickly your stormy sea can be silenced.

Baby Moses

Supplies: old bedsheet, baby doll

This is a fun way to teach the story of Moses in the basket (Exodus 2:1-10).

Let's Play

Cut an old sheet into a large circle. You'll also need a soft baby doll to represent baby Moses. Lay the sheet on the floor, and have the children sit around it in a circle. Say: **When Moses was a baby, his mother was frightened for his safety. So she hid him in a basket in the river.** Put the baby doll in the middle of the sheet, and have the children grasp the edges of the sheet with both hands.

Say: **While Moses was on the river, the waves gently rocked him to sleep. Let's make some gentle waves.** Have the children gently lift the sheet up and down to make waves.

Say: **Soldiers came to the river looking for all the baby boys in the land.** Have the children stand, hold the sheet up high, and look under it. Have children walk in a circle, looking back and forth. Then have children sit on the floor again, laying the sheet down.

Say: **One day a princess came to the river. She saw the baby and sent a servant to bring the baby to the shore.** Choose a child to "wade" across the sheet, pick up baby Moses and bring him to the shore. Say: **Later, the princess took Moses to the palace and cared for him while he grew up.**

Play again, and let several children bring baby Moses to the shore.

►Ark Relay

• • • • • • • • • • • • •

Supplies: paper grocery sack, scissors, markers, tape, glue stick, newsprint

Children will fill an "ark" during this lively game.

Let's Play

Before this activity, cut a paper grocery sack into several 1-inch squares to represent pieces of wood. Then draw a simple ark shape on a large sheet of newsprint. Refer to the illustration below. Tape the newsprint to a wall. Set the paper squares and a glue stick on a chair next to the ark.

Have the children form a line about 10 feet away from the newsprint. Say: **We're going to help Noah build his ark! When I say "go," the first person in line will hop to the ark, take a piece of "wood," rub glue on it, and stick it on the ark shape. Then he or she will hop back and let the next person have a turn. Ready? Go!**

Encourage children waiting in line to cheer on their classmates. You may want to instruct each child to travel to the ark in a different way, such as skipping, walking on tiptoes, walking backward, waddling like a duck, or crawling.

If you have more than eight children, make two arks and form two lines. However, don't make the game competitive—just let the kids play for fun.

Continue the game until the ark shape is filled in.

Fire Walkers

Supplies: none

This game is a great accompaniment to the story of Shadrach, Meshach, and Abednego in the fiery furnace (Daniel 3).

Let's Play

Form two groups. Have one group scatter around the middle of the room and sit down. Be sure these children are more than an arm's length apart. Direct the other group to stand against one wall.

Say: **In this Bible story, three men were thrown into a huge fire because they wouldn't worship a golden statue. Let's pretend that this group of kids in the middle is a big fire.**

Have those children raise their hands and wiggle their fingers like flames. They may want to make crackling and hissing noises as well.

Say: **Now let's see if this other group can carefully walk through the fire to the other wall without getting "burned." If one of the "flames" touches you, sit down and join the "fire."**

Give a signal, and have children start walking through the fire. Have the children who reach the opposite wall walk back, trying to keep clear of the flames.

Have kids play until one child is left, then have the groups switch roles.

Matching Gifts

Supplies: gift wrap, scissors, tape, small candy bars

This game works well at Christmas or on birthdays.

Let's Play

Wrap some small candy bars in scraps of different-colored gift wrap.

"Let's Play!"

Make sure you have one gift for each child. Also cut a small square from each of the different gift wraps you use.

Before class, hide the gifts around the room. When the children arrive, give them each a scrap of gift wrap, and have them hunt for the gift that is wrapped in matching paper. If some children can't find their gifts, have the rest of the class help them search.

Then enjoy unwrapping and eating the gifts together.

Lost Sheep

Supplies: none

Children love Hide-and-Seek activities. This one is especially versatile; you can use it for any Bible story with a shepherd reference.

Let's Play

Choose one child to be the "shepherd." Everyone else is a sheep. Have the sheep crawl around the room calling "Baa, baa."

Have the shepherd hide his or her eyes while you choose one sheep to hide. Then have everyone sing this song to the tune of "Ten Little Indians."

Where, oh where is little sheep hiding?
Where, oh where is little sheep hiding?
Where, oh where is little sheep hiding?
Shh, let's listen for him (or her).

At this point, have the lost sheep softly say "baa" while the other children are quiet.

The shepherd searches for the lost sheep. Have the other sheep baa softly when the shepherd is far away, and baa loudly when the shepherd gets close to the lost sheep.

When the sheep is found, it becomes the new shepherd and the shepherd becomes a sheep.

Have the children play until everyone has been either the shepherd or the lost sheep.

I Think I Can

Supplies: none

You'll have a grand time acting out this favorite children's story.

Let's Play

Using books and chairs, set up an obstacle course that winds around the room. Have the children form a "train" by standing in a line. Have each child hold the waist of the person in front of him or her. Have the train begin traveling around the room, making chugging noises.

Tell the first child in line, the engineer, to pretend to sound a train whistle. Have the engineer lead the train through the obstacle course. As the train faces each obstacle, have the children softly say, "I think I can; I think I can." As each obstacle is passed, have the children say, "I knew I could; I knew I could." Have the children play until the train passes by all the obstacles.

If you have time, choose another engineer and begin the game again.

I Love Jesus

Supplies: none

In this game, children will have fun jumping, playing, and saying "I love you" to Jesus.

Let's Play

Have two children hold hands and raise their arms to make a "bridge." Have the rest of the children line up, ready to walk under the bridge.

Lead the class in singing the following song to the tune of "London Bridge." While you're singing, have the children walk under the bridge. If you have a large group, you may want to sing this verse twice.

"Let's Play!"

Jesus made this happy day, happy day, happy day.
Jesus made this happy day so I can jump and play.

At the end of the verse, have the bridge lower its gates around the child who's walking underneath. Have that child make the following motions, while you sing the next verse.

Sing and jump and turn around, turn around, turn around.
Sing and jump and turn around. I love Jesus! *(Hug self and point to heaven.)*

Repeat the song several times to give all the children a chance to be caught in the bridge. Then have different children form a new bridge and play again.

Going on a Bear Hunt

Supplies: cardboard or poster board, markers, spray paint or flour

This is a great pretending game to play outside.

Let's Play

Draw a bear paw print on a 1×1-foot piece of cardboard or poster board and cut it out to create a stencil. Use the illustration below as a guide.

Before the children arrive, create a path on your church lawn by laying down the stencil every few feet and spray-painting the grass that shows through the holes. (The paint will disappear the next time the grass is cut.) If the grass is very short or if you're using an empty parking lot, then use flour to mark the path. At the end of the path, hide a treat such as tiny, bear-shaped crackers.

When the children arrive, take them on a "bear hunt." Have them creep and stalk the bear, following the paw prints to the treat. After the children enjoy the treat, have them sing a song such as "The Bear Went Over the Mountain" and run a bear race in which everyone must walk on all fours to the finish line.

Camel Run

Supplies: paper lunch sacks, jelly beans, tape or stapler
Celebrate the wise men's journey to Bethlehem (Matthew 2:1-12) with this game.

Let's Play

Before this activity, fill paper lunch sacks with small handfuls of jelly beans or some other treat. Fold the top of the bags down, then tape or staple them shut. You'll need a "treasure bag" for each child.

Form trios and say: **After Jesus was born, three wise men traveled a long way to bring him wonderful gifts. In this game, we can pretend to be wise men, bringing gifts on our camels! But first, you'll need to choose someone in your group to be the "camel."**

When the trios have chosen their camels, give each trio three treasure bags, and have everyone line up along one wall. Instruct the camels to get on their hands and knees. Have the two "wise men" stand on either side of the camels.

Tell the wise men to put one of their treasure bags on their camels' backs and put the other two bags on the floor. Have the camels crawl and the wise men walk as they carefully deliver their treasure bags to the opposite side of the room. Have the wise men help keep the bags

from falling off of the camels' backs. The wise men will set the bags on the floor, then the trios will travel back to get another treasure bag. Let a different child be the camel on each trip. Continue the game until all the treasure bags have been delivered.

After the game, have the trios sit together, open the bags, and enjoy their tasty treasures.

►Is It the Truth?

Supplies: none

Children will be challenged to tell the truth in this fast-paced game.

Let's Play

The goal of this game is to move forward to touch the "caller" standing across the room from the starting line.

An adult or teen volunteer can be the caller. The caller will stand on one side of the room with his or her back turned to the children. The caller can call out statements such as "Frogs hop" and "Five is a number."

The children stand on the opposite side of the room. If a statement is true, the children tiptoe toward the caller. If a statement (such as "ice is hot") is false, the children stand still. The caller can turn around after giving a false statement to see if any children are moving. Any children caught moving must go back to the starting line.

As children tag the caller, they can stand beside the caller or return to the starting line and play again.

►Help the Blind

Supplies: blindfold

Create a spirit of cooperation as children help each other in this game.

Let's Play

Form two groups, and have them line up so they each face each other. This is the "tunnel." Have the children stand with space between them so that the lines go from one end of the room to the other.

Blindfold the first child in one of the lines. Have him or her walk to the other end of the tunnel without running into any of the children. Have the children clap slowly and softly as the blindfolded child walks through the tunnel. If the blindfolded child comes too close to anyone, have the other children clap loudly and quickly. When the child reaches the end of the tunnel, lead the children in a rousing cheer. Then have the child join the end of the line, and blindfold the first child in the other line.

Play until every child has had a chance to go through the tunnel.

►Animal Riddles

Supplies: none

Children love riddles, and they'll have fun acting out the answers in this game.

Let's Play

Have the children scatter around the room. Read the following riddles aloud, and have the children call out the name of the animal you're

describing in each one. Then have them act like that animal as they travel once around the room.

- **I hop up and down, and I like to eat carrots. What am I?** (Children will say "bunny" and hop.)
- **I jump and I carry my babies in my pocket. What am I?** (Children will say "kangaroo" and jump.)
- **I hiss and stick out my tongue as I slither on the ground. Who am I?** (Children will say "snake" and wiggle.)
- **I'm big and gray, and I have a very long nose. What am I?** (Children will say "elephant," hold their arms out from their noses, and walk with heavy steps.)
- **I growl a lot, and I have a big mane. What am I?** (Children will say "lion," crawl on all fours, and growl.)

Older preschoolers will enjoy thinking of more animal riddles to tell to the class.

Joseph's Coat

Supplies: paper grocery sacks, scissors, washable markers, cassette player, tape of praise music

Children each make their own "coat of many colors" in this creative game. Use this activity with lessons on Joseph (Genesis 37).

Let's Play

Cut slits up the fronts of paper grocery bags. Cut neck holes in the top of the bags and armholes in the sides to make "coats." Make a coat for each child.

Have each child put on a paper coat, and give each child a washable marker. Be sure the markers are water based and won't bleed through the paper onto clothing.

Play praise music and have the children march around the room. Stop the music and have each child find a partner. Have partners draw simple designs on each other's coats. After a few seconds of drawing, start the music again.

Continue until the children's coats are full of colorful designs.

Rag Doll, Toy Soldier

Supplies: none

Children will love acting like toys in this imaginative game.

Let's Play

Have the children scatter around the room. Call out, "rag doll," and have the children walk as if they were rag dolls. They might flop their arms and heads or walk unsteadily. After a bit, call out, "toy soldier," and have the children march stiffly, as if they were toy soldiers.

Play for several minutes, alternating calls of "rag doll" and "toy soldier."

If you have older preschoolers, give each child a turn being the caller. You may wish to call out the names of other toys, or use animal names to give a different twist to the game.

The Eye of the Needle

Supplies: none

This game will help children understand what Jesus told the rich young man (Mark 10:25).

Let's Play

Have the children stand in a line, one behind the other, with their legs spread to form a tunnel.

Say: **Jesus said that it is easier for a camel to go through the eye of a needle than it is for a rich man to enter the kingdom of God. Let's pretend that we're camels with humps and we're trying to get through the tiny eye of a needle.**

Have the last child in line drop to his or her knees and crawl through the tunnel, or "eye of the needle." When the child gets through

69

the tunnel, he or she will stand up, join the line, and say, "This camel made it." That's the signal for the next child at the back of the line to drop to his or her knees and crawl through the eye of the needle.

Play for several minutes. See how fast the children can thread their way through the needle.

Plant a Garden

Supplies: none

Young children are fascinated with seeds and gardens. They'll enjoy pretending to grow from seeds into plants in this game.

Let's Play

Choose one child to be the "farmer." Everyone else is a "seed." Have all the seeds huddle together in a tight group.

One by one the farmer takes each seed by the hand and leads it to a separate spot in the room. As the farmer delivers each seed, he or she gently taps the seed on the head to plant it, and the seed crouches on the floor.

When the "garden" has been planted, the farmer hurries from one seed to the next, pretending to pour water on each one. As each seed is watered, it jumps up and waves its arms like a plant swaying in the breeze. The plants keep swaying in the breeze until the last seed is watered. The last seed to "sprout" becomes the new farmer for another round of play.

Let the children continue playing until everyone has been the farmer.

The Nature Game

Supplies: blanket

This simplified scavenger hunt is a great game to play in a field or a park. Just make sure children have adequate supervision and don't stray near streets or parking lots.

Let's Play

You'll need a blanket or a picnic table to use as a display area.

Have children form pairs. Give the pairs one minute to look for the first item on the list below, "something green." As they bring back their green items, have the children examine what other pairs found. When everyone has returned, send the children in search of the second item. Continue until all the items have been found. At the end of the game, thank God for the wonders of his creation.

Here are examples of what the children might look for:
- something green
- something wooden
- something smooth
- something bumpy
- something with more than one color
- something pretty
- something dirty
- something wet
- something sandy

Feel free to change the items on your list to suit your environment.

Windows

Supplies: none

Your children will "fly" in this fanciful game.

Let's Play

Choose one child to be the "bird." Have everyone else join hands and stand in a circle with arms raised high to create "open windows."

Have the bird walk, skip, or hop in and out of the open windows all the way around the circle. Encourage the children to whistle or tweet as the bird "flies" about. After the bird "flies" in or out of each window, have those children lower their arms to close the window.

After the bird has flown all the way around the circle and all the windows are closed, have him or her join the circle. Choose another child to be the bird and begin the game again. Continue playing until every child has had a turn to be the bird.

Rhythmic Good News

Supplies: none

This game introduces children to telling others about God's love.

Let's Play

Have the children sit in a circle. Say: **We have good news to tell the rest of the world: God loves us! Let's have fun spreading the news!**

Clap your hands as you say to the child on your right, "God loves you." Have that child clap his or her hands and give the message to the next child. Continue all the way around the circle.

Then change the action that you use to spread the message. For example, you might pat your head, hop up and down, or push your cheeks together to form fish lips. Have the children think of actions, too.

Older preschoolers will enjoy thinking of other good-news messages to spread around the circle, such as "Jesus is alive," "Jesus died for us," or "God takes care of us."

Land, Water, Sky

Supplies: tape; pictures of a field, ocean, and sky

Help children develop critical thinking skills with this active sorting game.

Let's Play

Tape magazine pictures of a field, an ocean, and the sky to three separate walls in your classroom.

Have the children stand in the middle of the room. Call out various animals, birds, and insects. Have the children first determine whether that creature lives on the land, in the water, or in the sky. Then have them walk or hop to the appropriate picture. Remember that in some cases, more than one answer is correct. Continue calling out animal names for several minutes.

To make this a high-energy game, have the children imitate the animal as they move to the pictures.

Tentmakers

Supplies: one bath towel and two chairs for every child

All children love to make tents, so this game is sure to be a hit. Use it with lessons on outreach or the early church.

Let's Play

To begin the game, lay the chairs on their sides and scatter them around the room. Scatter the towels on the floor near the chairs.

Say: **Paul was a missionary, but he was also a tentmaker. Let's make a big tent to enjoy together.**

Have the group work together to create a tent that's big enough for everyone to sit under. Have the children bring the chairs close together,

73

stand them up, and drape the bath towels over them. When the tent's finished, have everyone climb inside for a short story or song.

Patterns

Supplies: paper, colorful markers

This game is a lot of fun for children who are learning to identify colors.

Let's Play

Draw scribble pictures of different colors on sheets of paper, one color per sheet. Make two pictures of each color and put them in two piles. Hand one set of color pictures to the children, one picture per child.

Set out three pictures on the floor from your set. Have the children whose colors you've set out line up next to those pictures.

Then gather the pictures and set out three more pictures. Play until you've set out all of the pictures.

End the game by putting all of the color pictures in one line on the floor. Have the children line up next to their corresponding color pictures.

The Beautiful Feet That Bring Good News

Supplies: index cards, markers

Have the children take off their shoes and socks for this toe-wiggling game about delivering good news (Isaiah 52:7, King James Version).

Let's Play

Draw a heart or write the words "Good News!" on an index card, and fold the card in half. Form two groups and have them line up on opposite sides of the room.

Say: **The Bible says that beautiful feet bring good news. Let's deliver the good news with our feet.**

Give the card to the first person in one of the lines. Have the child put the card between his or her toes and walk across the room. Then have the child give the card to the first person in the other line and go to the back of that line. Then that child will walk across the room with the card between his or her toes, give the card to the next person in the other line, and join the back of that line.

If the card falls from between a child's toes, have him or her replace it, but don't insist that the child start over.

Continue until everyone has had at least one turn to deliver the good news.

Share!

Supplies: envelopes, cereal loops or raisins

Children will find that sharing is fun in this game.

Let's Play

Give each child an envelope and put several cereal loops or raisins in each one. Don't seal the envelopes.

Have the children hand out their cereal loops to one another. Tell the children that the goal of the game is to get rid of all their loops, but they must accept the loops that others give to them.

Play for several minutes. Then have the children each empty their envelopes in a pile in front of them. Ask the children what happens when they share with others.

Save the "used" cereal for the birds, and give each child a handful of fresh cereal loops to nibble.

Naaman's Spots

Supplies: washtub, soapy water, washable markers, paper towels
Bring the story of Naaman alive with this game (2 Kings 5:1-4).

Let's Play

Fill a small washtub or a small children's swimming pool with soapy water. Use a washable marker to put colored dots on each child's hands.

Say: **When Naaman was covered with spots, the prophet Elisha told him to dip his body in the Jordan river seven times. Let's see what happened to him.**

Have the children plunge their hands under the water and scrub gently. Caution the children not to touch their eyes with their soapy hands. Have the children lift their hands at the same time you do, and have everyone call out, "One!"

Have the children plunge their hands in the water again and scrub gently. Then have them lift their hands together again, and have everyone call out, "Two!"

Continue seven times. Then look for the spots. Say: **Our spots are gone! Naaman's spots were gone, too, because God healed him.**

Provide paper towels so the children can dry their hands.

Balancing Act

Supplies: round containers, cardboard, tennis or Ping-Pong balls
This is a great partnership game for older preschoolers.

Let's Play

For every two children, you'll need a round cardboard container such as an oatmeal box, a ball, and a piece of cardboard that's as wide as the

oatmeal box and about 2 feet long.

Form pairs. Have each pair put the oatmeal box on its side and position the cardboard on top of it. Then have them balance the ball on the cardboard while they gently tip the cardboard back and forth like a seesaw.

For more fun, blow a whistle every 30 seconds, and have the children switch partners.

Cast the Net

Supplies: small towel

Children pretend to be fish in this game, which can be used with a variety of Bible stories.

Let's Play

Play with an uneven number of people. Choose one child to be the "fisherman." Form two equal-sized groups and have them scatter and crouch down on opposite sides of the room.

Put a row of chairs in the middle of the room, and line them up so the seats of the chairs are facing the back of the chairs in front of them. Include one chair for every child in a group. For example, if you have five children on each side of the room, use five chairs. The row of chairs represents the boat.

Have the fisherman sit in the first chair in the boat. Give the child a small towel to wave on both sides of the boat. Then have the child drop the towel on one side of the boat, and have all the "fish" on that side take a seat on the boat. The child left without a seat on the boat becomes the fisherman for the next round.

77

Continue the game for several minutes and make sure both sides of the boat get equal playtime.

Angel Wings

Supplies: feathers

This game is a fun variation of the game Seven Up.

Let's Play

Show the children how to lightly brush someone's forearm with a feather, and say: **Let's pretend that this is what it feels like to be brushed with an angel's wing.**

Choose one-fourth to one-third of your children to be "angels," and have them stand at the front of the room. Give each of them a feather.

Have the other children lie face down on the floor with their eyes closed and their faces hidden in the crook of their elbows.

Have the angels each quietly walk through the room and lightly brush one child's forearm. As soon as they've brushed someone's arm, have the angels return to the front of the room and put their feathers down.

When the angels have all returned to the front of the room, have the other children sit up. If they were brushed by an "angel's wing," have them stand up. One by one, call on them to identify who they think touched them. If they're right, they trade places with the angel who touched them. If they're wrong, then the children who touched them are angels for another round of the game.

Have the children play until everyone has been brushed by an angel's wing or until everyone has had a chance to be an angel.

78

Active Games

The Tail of the Whale

Supplies: none

This unique chasing game will go over "swimmingly."

Let's Play

Have the children stand in a line and hold on to the waists of the children in front of them. Tell the children to pretend that they're a big whale swishing through the ocean.

The person at the head of the whale will try to catch the tail of the whale by tagging the person at the back of the line. Encourage all of the children to hold on tightly as the whale twists and turns. When the "tail" is finally tagged, have the first child in line become the new tail. Have the second person in line become the new "head," and start the game over. Continue until each child has had a chance to be the head of the whale.

Fish Flop

Supplies: colorful construction paper, tape, markers

Play this active game when your lesson is about the disciples who were fishermen.

Let's Play

Draw fish shapes on several different colors of construction paper. Use three or four colors, and be sure to make one fish in each color for each child. Write the word "Jesus" on another sheet of construction paper and tape it to the wall.

Scatter the fish shapes on the floor around the room. Have the children stand around the room. Call out different colors and have the children each jump on a fish of that color. After you've called out several

colors, say, "Follow Jesus!" and have the children "swim" over to the word "Jesus."

After the game, talk about how the first disciples left everything they had to follow Jesus.

Take a Trip

Supplies: "Transportation Cards" handout (p. 82), two boxes, paper, pen

Use this game when you teach about Paul's missionary trips or your church's outreach programs.

Let's Play

This game works best in a large room or on a grassy field. If you play this game outside, clearly define boundaries to keep children from getting hurt or wandering off.

Cut apart the cards from the "Transportation Cards" handout, and put them in a box. Then write the numbers 1 through 5 on separate slips of paper, and put them in another small box.

Say: **Let's go on a missionary trip just as Paul and Barnabas did. We'll tell the good news of Jesus on our journey, and we can travel in lots of exciting and different ways.**

Have the children line up shoulder to shoulder at one end of the playing area. Have a child choose a slip of paper from each box, and read the slips to the class. For example, the child might draw "boats" and "3." Put the slips back in the boxes. Have that child lead the rest of the children as they pretend to paddle boats to the opposite side of the playing area. Then have them each say to three people, "Jesus loves you." If a child draws "swimming" and "two," the children pretend to swim across the room and each tell two people that Jesus loves them.

Continue playing until every child has had a chance to choose slips of paper.

Transportation Cards

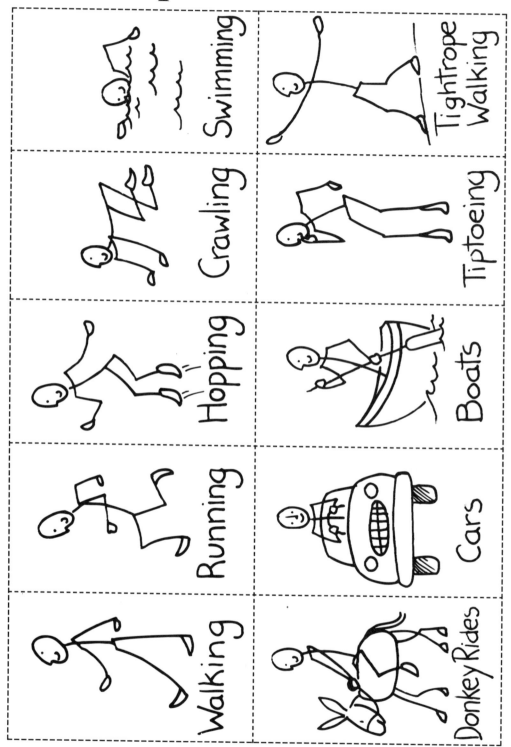

Swimming

Tightrope Walking

Crawling

Tiptoeing

Hopping

Boats

Running

Cars

Walking

Donkey Rides

Scatter, Sparrows!

Supplies: none

The Bible tells us that God does not forget even a sparrow!
The children will enjoy pretending to be sparrows (Psalm 84).

Let's Play

Form pairs and give these directions: "Touch feet," "Touch wings," and
"Tweet to your partner." Then call out: **Scatter, sparrows!** Have the
children flap their wings as they hurry to find new partners. Repeat similar directions, then have the children scatter again. Have them play the
game several times.

Company's Coming

Supplies: none

This game works well with lessons about Mary and Martha
(Luke 10:38-42).

Let's Play

Explain that when Jesus came to Mary and Martha's house, Martha hurried and scurried to clean the house and prepare a good meal. Mary
was different—she sat quietly and listened to Jesus.

Say: **When I call out "Martha," pretend to tidy and polish
our room. When I call out "Mary," drop to the floor and sit
quietly.**

Call out the names "Mary" and "Martha" several times, and have the
children act out the roles.

You can also use this game to tidy your room before story time. Call
out "Martha," and have children straighten the room. Call out "Mary" as
you gather the children for the lesson.

83

on Praise

balloons, tape, permanent marker, cassette player, tape of praise music

This praise game is a lot of fun for older preschoolers who know their letters.

Let's Play

Inflate nine balloons. Use a permanent marker to write one letter from the phrase "Praise God" on each balloon. Stick nine tape loops to the wall at kids' eye level so the balloons can be fastened to the wall later.

Distribute the balloons among the children. It's not necessary for every child to have one. If you have fewer than nine children, have some children hold more than one. If you have more than nine children, have them work in pairs.

Say: **When you hear the music, bat the balloons to each other. When the music stops, catch a balloon. If you don't catch a balloon, stand next to someone who has one.**

Play lively praise music, and have the children bat the balloons. After a short while, stop the music and have the children catch the balloons. When all the balloons have been caught, ask: **Who has a balloon with the letter "P" on it?** Have that child or those children put that balloon on the first piece of tape.

Start the music again. When it stops, ask for the letter "R," and have that child put the balloon on the second piece of tape.

Continue until the balloons on the wall spell "Praise God."

Help the students read the phrase and shout, "Praise God" together.

Butterflies and Caterpillars

Supplies: none

This is an exciting game to play in the springtime—or any time children need to get the wiggles out.

Let's Play

Say: **When I call out "butterflies," pretend you are a butterfly, and fly around the room. When I call out "caterpillars," drop to the floor, and crawl like a caterpillar.**

Play the game for several minutes, calling out "butterflies" and "caterpillars" every few seconds.

Try using other springtime words such as "eggs" and "chicks" to add variety.

Raven Bread

Supplies: plastic bowls, small crackers, paper cups, picture of Elijah

Use this game when you're teaching about Elijah and the ravens (1 Kings 17:1-6).

Let's Play

Set out a plastic bowl of oyster crackers or small cheese crackers on one side of the room. On the other side of the room, place an empty plastic bowl and a picture of Elijah or a doll that can represent Elijah.

Say: **Elijah was hungry, so God sent birds called ravens to give bread to Elijah. Let's pretend we're ravens bringing bread to Elijah.**

85

"Let's Play!"

Give each child a paper cup with a cracker in it. Have the children one by one hold their cups with their mouths, "fly" across the room, and empty their cups into the other bowl. Encourage them to flap their wings and caw like crows as they deliver the crackers. Continue the game until each child has delivered several crackers.

Pass around the bowl of unused crackers for children to enjoy. Save the crackers from the game to feed the "outdoor" birds.

David and Jonathan Partners

Supplies: cassette player, tape of praise music

Preschoolers are just beginning to enjoy friendships outside the family. They'll have fun being friends in this game.

Let's Play

Form pairs and have them link arms or hold hands. Say: **David and Jonathan were friends who did lots of things together. We can have fun doing things together too.**

Play lively praise music and call out actions for the pairs to perform together, such as "march," "hop," "walk backward," "tiptoe," and "jump."

Periodically stop the music, and have the children find new partners. Then start the music again and call out more actions. Have the children play for several minutes.

Daniel, the Lions Are Coming

Supplies: none

Have the children play this game when your story is "Daniel and the Lions" (Daniel 6).

Let's Play

Choose one child to be "Daniel." Have Daniel stand on the far side of the room with his back turned to the rest of the class. Have the other children pretend to be lions. They will quietly creep up and try to touch Daniel before Daniel hears them. If Daniel hears a noise, he will turn around and point to the lion who made the noise. If Daniel guesses correctly, that lion must go back to the starting place. The first lion to touch Daniel gets a big hug from him and becomes the next Daniel.

Continue this game until several children have been Daniel.

Jesus' Footsteps

Supplies: paper, marker, paper cutter, pair of shoes

This is a game that travels well. Use it to move children from place to place or just to have fun in your classroom.

Let's Play

Trace a pair of shoes on a piece of paper. Photocopy the paper, and cut the copies in half with a paper cutter. Create a path, setting the footprints a few feet apart. Your path can lead children under tables, over chairs, and around boxes.

After the children have followed the path you've created, they'll have

87

fun setting up their own trails for each other.

If you're working with young preschoolers, divide the footprints among them. Older children can work with all of the footprints.

►Part the Sea

Supplies: none

This game ties in well with the story of Moses and the Israelites escaping from Egypt (Exodus 12-15).

Let's Play

Choose one child to be Moses. Have the rest of the class line up behind Moses. Have Moses say, "God was good; he parted the sea. Come on, Israelites, follow me!"

Have Moses choose an action to lead the other children around the room. Encourage the other children to imitate Moses as they follow him once around the room. Then choose another child to be Moses.

Play until everyone has had a chance to be Moses.

►Color Hop

Supplies: none

This game is great when you're teaching about Joseph's coat of many colors (Genesis 37).

Let's Play

Lead the children in this song about colors. Sing it to the tune of "Old MacDonald."

I see something that is (color).
Do you see it too?

I see something that is (same color).
Hop there if you do!

With a hop, hop here
And a hop, hop there.
Hurry up! Hop it up!
Hop as fast as you dare.

I see something that is (color).
Do you see it too?

Have the children tell you what they've found that matches the color you've named. Play several times, naming a different color each time. Older children will enjoy being the leaders.

►The Gleaning Game

Supplies: scissors; markers or crayons; paper lunch sacks; red, yellow, and blue construction paper

This just-for-fun game goes well with any lesson on Ruth.

Let's Play

Before this activity, cut 1-inch squares from red, yellow, and blue construction paper. You'll need about 40 squares of each color. Then use markers or crayons to color three paper lunch sacks, one to match each of the construction paper colors. Set each bag in a different corner of the room.

Scatter the paper squares all over the floor, mixing the colors well. Then form three groups, and assign each group to one of the three colors. You may want to use a marker to put colored dots on the children's hands so they can remember their colors.

Say: **In this game, pretend you're like Ruth, gathering pieces of wheat for your supper. You can only gather the paper pieces of wheat that match your group's color. So if you're in the red group, only gather the red wheat. After you've gathered a handful, take giant steps to your team's colored bag and place**

the wheat inside. When your group can't find any more wheat that is your color, sit down near your bag. Are you ready? Let's go!

As children gather the wheat, be sure they take giant steps rather than run. When everyone is seated, have the children scatter the wheat and play again.

Big Fish, Little Fish, Free Fish!

Supplies: jump-ropes

Play this variation of Tag when your lesson is about fish or fishermen.

Let's Play

Use jump-ropes to form two circular "fish nets" on the floor on opposite sides of the room.

Choose two children to be fishermen, and say: **Jesus had many friends who were fishermen. They caught lots of fish, and then they sold the fish in the market for people to eat. Let's play a game about fish. When I call out, "Big fish, little fish, swim, swim, swim!" everyone will run from the fishermen. If a fisherman tags you, go stand inside one of the fish nets. When the nets get too crowded, I'll call out, "Big fish, little fish, swim away free!" Then you can all escape and play again.**

Play for several minutes. Change fishermen often.

Disciple Tag

Supplies: none

Children can play this game when you're teaching about being a disciple of Jesus.

Let's Play

Choose one child to be a "disciple." Have the other children scatter around the room or field. When the disciple tags someone, that person will become a disciple too. Then both disciples will try to tag the other children. Disciples must tiptoe, and no one may run. Continue until all the children have become disciples.

After the game, you may want to talk about some of the things Jesus' disciples did and what people who follow Jesus today can do.

Hurricane Watch!

Supplies: balloons

Children will love turning the room into a wild, stormy sea in this game.

Let's Play

Before this activity, inflate and tie off at least one balloon per child.

Give each child a balloon, and say: **Let's make the stormy sea that Jesus calmed. When I say "Storm!" toss your balloons up in the air, and bop them around. We'll turn our room into a wild, stormy sea! Then I'll call out, "Be still." That's what Jesus said to make the storm stop. When I say, "Be still," grab your balloons, and sit down quickly and quietly.**

As you play this game, encourage the children to bop their balloons

upward, rather than toward others. Explain that you want to make tall waves. If any of the balloons pop, toss a new one into the "storm" so that each child has a balloon to snatch when it's time to sit down.

Roll the Rock

Supplies: none

This is a fun outdoor game to play during the Easter season. If you play inside, move the furniture out of the way.

Let's Play

Form two groups, and have them line up on opposite sides of the room.

Say: **When the women came to visit Jesus' tomb, they were surprised to find the stone had been rolled away from the doorway. Jesus' body wasn't there because he was alive! In this game, we'll be rolled away, just as the stone was.**

Have the first child in one of the groups lie down with his or her arms over his or her head. On "go" have the child roll across the room toward the other group. When he or she reaches the other side of the room, have the child stand and go to the rear of the second group's line.

Have the first child in the second group roll across the room to the first group. You may need to help the children stay on course.

Continue until everyone has had at least one turn.

Follow the Light

Supplies: flashlight

Play this game when you discuss Jesus as the light of the world or when you talk about following Jesus.

Let's Play

Have the children skip and follow the beam of a flashlight as you shine it all over the room. Make the flashlight beam dance on the floor and skip from wall to wall. Have the children jump to touch the beam as you shine it high. Have them follow the beam under tables and around chairs. After the children have chased the light for a while, sing this song with the children to the tune of "Row, Row, Row Your Boat."

> Jesus is the light
> Over all the world.
> I will love and follow him.
> Wherever I may go.

Older preschoolers will enjoy taking turns with the flashlight.

Gone Fishing

Supplies: scissors, tissue paper, masking tape, bathroom-tissue tubes
Use this game when you study any New Testament story that mentions fishing.

Let's Play

Cut plenty of fish from tissue paper. Use the picture below as a guide. Make two masking tape lines about 10 feet apart. Tell the children that one masking tape line is a fish net. Put all the tissue paper fish behind the other line, and have the children blow through empty bathroom-tissue tubes to make the fish move toward the net.

As the children get their fish to the net, have them hurry back to the other line to "catch" more fish.

93

Mix and Match

Supplies: old greeting cards, scissors

This game is a great way to form pairs. Use it as an ice-breaker or to welcome new children to your class.

Let's Play

You'll need the front of an old greeting card for every two children. Before class, cut each of the greeting card fronts into two puzzle pieces.

When the children arrive, give each child a puzzle piece. Call out an action such as "walk," "hop," "shuffle," or "jump," and have the children do that action while you lead this song to the tune of "Oh Where, Oh Where Has My Little Dog Gone?"

Oh where, oh where has my dear friend gone?
Oh where, oh where can she be?
Oh where, oh where has my dear friend gone?
Oh where, oh where can he be?

When the song ends, each child tries to match his or her puzzle piece to someone else's. When everyone has found a match, have the children switch pieces to play again.

Arky, Arky

Supplies: masking tape

This is a fun game based on the story of Noah's ark.

Let's Play

Use masking tape to make an ark shape on the floor in a corner of

94

your room. Refer to the drawing below for guidance. The ark shape should be large enough so all children can stand inside it.

Choose one child to be "Noah." Have the rest of the children choose an animal sound to make. When you say, "It looks like rain," have all the children wander around the room making their animal sounds. Have Noah touch each child one by one on the shoulder. As Noah tags the children, have them walk into the ark.

You may want to stand by the ark and sprinkle the children with confetti "rain" as they enter the ark. When all the animals are in the ark, Noah will step inside the ark too. Then choose another Noah and begin the game again.

For extra fun, have the children move like animals as they make animal sounds.

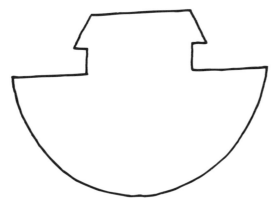

Wave Race

Supplies: wading pool, water, plastic spoons, Ping-Pong ball

This is a cool outdoor game for a hot day.

Let's Play

Fill a small wading pool with water. Give each child a plastic spoon. Drop a Ping-Pong ball in the middle of the pool. On "go" have all the children try to get the ball to the opposite side of the pool by making waves with their spoons.

Children may not touch the ball or other children with their spoons. They also may not intentionally splash other children.

95

Don't encourage the class to play this game to win—just to cool off and have fun!

Vary the game for older preschoolers, who will enjoy being the first to "spoon up" the ball.

►Big Fish

Supplies: none

Use this game when you teach your children the story of Jonah.

Let's Play

Have the children sit in a circle. Teach them this rhyme:

Big fish, big fish in the sea,
You caught Jonah
But you can't catch me!

Then choose someone to be "It," who circles behind the children as they repeat the rhyme. When the children say the word "me," It will gently tap the nearest child. The child who is tapped will become the big fish and will chase It around the circle and back to the empty space. If It gets to the space first, then the big fish is the new It. If the big fish tags It, then he or she remains It for the next round.

Have the children play until several children get a chance to be It.

►Gathering Sheep

Supplies: cotton balls, newspapers

This game is fun to play during any lesson that includes sheep or shepherds.

96

Let's Play

Scatter a package of cotton balls on the floor all over the room. Designate one corner of the room as the "sheep pen."

Give each child a rolled newspaper tube, and have the children gather the "sheep" into the pen by "sweeping" them with the tubes. Play until all the sheep are safely home in the sheep pen.

For a variation, have the children try blowing the sheep into their pen!

Feather Toss

Supplies: craft feather or facial tissue

In this game, children quickly change from doing actions to standing quietly.

Let's Play

Have the children scatter around the room. Call out one of the actions below and toss a feather or facial tissue into the air. Have all the children do the action while the feather floats in the air. When the feather touches the ground, have the children freeze in place. Then toss the feather again, and call out another action. Try these actions and sounds.

- cry
- laugh
- sing
- jump
- skip
- walk like a robot
- crawl
- rub your tummy

Build the Wall

Supplies: building blocks, masking tape

This game is just right for teaching the story of Nehemiah.

Let's Play

You'll need a lot of blocks for this game. Big cardboard blocks work best, but if you don't have them in your room, you can make some by folding down the pointed ends of empty half-gallon milk cartons and taping them securely.

Pile the blocks in a row at one end of the room. Have children line up next to the row of blocks. If you have more than 10 children, form two groups and put the blocks between the two groups. Put a masking tape line on the opposite side of the room.

On "go" have the first child in line pick up a block, hop across the room, and set the block on the finish line. The first child will hop to the back of the line, and the second child will pick up a block, hop across the room, and put the block on the finish line next to the first block.

When every child has put a block on the finish line, have the children build a second layer of the wall. When the second row is complete, have the class work on a third row and keep building until the wall is several rows tall.

Have the class celebrate its building project with a loud "Hooray!"

Watch Out for the Whale

Supplies: none

Excitement grows as the whale in this game grows bigger and bigger!

Let's Play

Designate a playing area as the "ocean," and show the children where the boundaries are on each side. Make sure there's plenty of room to play this game, and caution children to speed walk rather than run.

Choose one child to be the "whale." Have the whale try to tag the children as they pretend to swim in the ocean. When a child is tagged, have him or her gently hold the waist of the whale. As more children are tagged, the whale will grow longer!

Continue until all of the children have been tagged and have formed one big whale. After the last child joins the whale, have the group break apart. The last child to be tagged becomes the new whale.

Snowball Fight

Supplies: lunch sacks, cotton balls or packing peanuts, masking tape, timer

No one will get cold during this snowball fight!

Let's Play

Form two groups and have them stand on opposite sides of a masking tape line.

Give each child a lunch sack full of cotton balls or foam packing peanuts. Have the children pretend the cotton balls are snowballs.

Set a timer for three minutes, and have the children throw their snowballs at the opposite group.

When the timer sounds, have the children pretend to shovel the snow by sweeping the cotton balls into a big pile with their hands.

Gather the snowballs in a sack, and save them to play the game again.

Fish Net

Supplies: none

This game is fishy fun for all involved.

Let's Play

Choose one child to be the "fish." Have the other children form a "net" by standing in a circle and holding hands. Have the fish stand in the middle of the circle and try to escape by "swimming" between people or breaking through their hands. Give the fish about 30 seconds to escape the net. If the fish breaks free, have all of the other children drop hands and swim to tag him or her. Then choose a new fish to stand inside the net. If the fish doesn't break through the net in 30 seconds, call time and choose a new fish.

Giants and Grasshoppers

Supplies: none

This Tag variation is based on Numbers 13.

Let's Play

Form two groups, the "grasshoppers" and the "giants." The grasshoppers must squat low and hop around the room. Their job is to tag the giants. The giants must walk around the room taking giant steps. When a grasshopper tags a giant, the grasshopper turns into a giant, and the giant turns into a grasshopper.

Have the children play for several minutes. If your grasshoppers get tired of hopping, then stop the game, and have the grasshoppers and giants trade places.

Scramble

Supplies: none

This game is great fun for kids who've learned to count to 10.

Let's Play

Make a circle of chairs facing out. You should have one less chair than you have children in your class.

Choose one child to be "It" and to stand in the middle of the circle. Say the first four lines of this verse while the other children march around the chairs. Then have the child in the middle count to 10.

Circle of chairs, circle of chairs.
I'd like a seat in the circle of chairs.
How long 'til I sit again?
Just until I count to 10!

One, two, three...

When the child gets to 10, everyone scrambles for a seat. The child left standing becomes the new It.

Doctor! Doctor!

Supplies: cardboard tubes

This game will show children what happens to their hearts when they exercise.

Let's Play

Give each child an empty cardboard tube. Form pairs, and have the children listen to their partners' hearts through the tubes. Then call out an

active motion such as "jumping jacks" or "jump." After the children exercise for a few seconds, call out, "Doctor! Doctor!" Have the children stop moving and listen to their partners' hearts through the tubes again.

Then have the children switch partners and do another active motion. Play for several minutes.

Thunder, Wind, and Lightning Bolts

Supplies: spray bottle with water

Create a storm in your classroom with this game.

Let's Play

Form three groups, the "thunder," the "wind," and the "lightning bolts." Have the children move around the room and act out their roles to create a terrifying storm. Have the thunder crash and kaboom. Have the wind blow. Have the lightning bolts strike by jumping and shaking.

After a few minutes, cool off the storm with the rain: Use a spray bottle to gently mist water over the children's heads. Then have the children switch roles and play again.

Tissue Throw

Supplies: facial tissues

This slow race is a lot of fun and is a perfect cure for those "rainy-day blues."

Let's Play

Have the children line up along a starting line. Designate a finish line about 20 feet away. Give each child a facial tissue. On "go" have children throw their tissues as far as they can. Then have the children hop to where their tissues landed, pick them up, and throw them again. Have the children continue throwing the tissues until they reach the finish line.

For round 2, let children blow their tissues along the floor to the finish line.

Songs and Finger Plays

Then and Now

Supplies: none

Preschoolers are growing and changing every day, and this song teaches that God can make all things new and different. Lead children in this simple action song to the tune of "Ten Little Indians."

Let's Play

I was sad *(make a sad face)*, but now I'm glad. *(Make a glad face.)*
I was sad *(make a sad face)*, but now I'm glad. *(Make a glad face.)*
I was sad *(make a sad face)*, but now I'm glad. *(Make a glad face.)*
God has made me glad.

I was small *(crouch down)*, but now I'm tall. *(Stand tall.)*
I was small *(crouch down)*, but now I'm tall. *(Stand tall.)*
I was small *(crouch down)*, but now I'm tall. *(Stand tall.)*
God helped me grow tall.

I used to crawl *(crawl)*, but now I walk. *(Walk in place.)*
I used to crawl *(crawl)*, but now I walk. *(Walk in place.)*
I used to crawl *(crawl)*, but now I walk. *(Walk in place.)*
God helped me to walk.

Lots of Food

Supplies: none

This silly song will help children learn about life on the ark.

Let's Play

Have the children sit in a circle. Say: **When Noah was on the ark with the animals, it was his job to make sure that the animals had enough food to eat. Let's help Noah feed the animals.**

Teach the children this simple song to the tune of "The Mulberry Bush."

Noah needed lots of food,
Lots of food, lots of food.
Noah needed lots of food
To feed all the animals.

After singing the song once or twice, point to a child and ask: **What animal did Noah feed?**

Point to another child and ask: **What food did Noah give to that animal?**

Use the children's responses to make the next verse of the song. For example, your song might sound like this:

Noah fed the goats spaghetti,
Goats spaghetti, goats spaghetti.
Noah fed the goats spaghetti.
The goats ate it up. Yum!

Encourage the children to come up with silly answers to the questions. Have everyone pretend to feed the animals while singing the song. And have the children rub their tummies while they say the word "yum." Continue until every child has chosen an animal or a type of food.

I Went to the Farm

Supplies: none

This is a fun game to play when your lesson is about Creation or Noah's ark.

Let's Play

Gather the children in a circle and sit down. Say this rhyme with the children. When you come to the first blank, point to a child who will name an animal. When you come to the second blank, have all the children make the noise that animal makes.

> I went to the farm. *(Make fingers walk.)*
> And what did I see? *(Point to eyes.)*
> I saw a _____,
> Who was smiling at me. *(Draw a smile on your face with your finger.)*
> I looked him in the eye. *(Point to eyes.)*
> Then I said, "Good day." *(Wave.)*
> And he said "_____" in his own special way.

God Made Us a World So Fair

Supplies: none

Children can play this game with hand motions sitting. Or, for a higher level of activity, they can walk around the room as they sing.

Let's Play

Sing this song to the tune of "Mary Had a Little Lamb."

> God made us a world so fair *(point to heaven),*
> World so fair, world so fair. *(Form a hoop with arms.)*
> God made us a world so fair. *(Point to heaven.)*
> We'll go walking there. *(Move fingers as if walking.)*
>
> The sun shines brightly overhead *(hold hands form a circle above head),*

Overhead, overhead. (*Hold hands form a circle above head.*)
The sun shines brightly overhead. (*Hold hands form a circle above head.*)
And on the flower beds. (*Point to the floor.*)

The grass is green beneath our feet (*wiggle toes*),
Beneath our feet, beneath our feet. (*Wiggle toes.*)
The grass is green beneath our feet. (*Wiggle toes.*)
The air smells very sweet. (*Sniff the air.*)

Raindrops falling all around (*wiggle fingers*),
All around, all around. (*Wiggle fingers.*)
Raindrops falling all around (*wiggle fingers*),
Splashing on the ground. (*Jump once as if in a puddle.*)

I see birds up in the trees (*flap arms*),
In the trees, in the trees. (*Extend arms as branches.*)
I see birds up in the trees. (*Flap arms.*)
God made all of these. (*Point to heaven.*)

If you have time, have the children tell you other things that God has created, and make up additional verses to the song.

Two by Two With Noah

Supplies: none

This is a fun "Noah's ark" song. Follow this song by telling the Bible story (Genesis 6:9–8:22).

Let's Play

Sing this song to the tune of "Eency, Weency Spider."

Two by two the animals marched into the ark. *(March in place.)*

Down came the rain, and the sky got very dark. *(Wiggle fingers for rain.)*

Out came the sun and dried up all the rain. *(Circle arms overhead for sun.)*

So Noah and the animals could walk the land again. *(Walk with fingers.)*

Three Little Wise Men

Supplies: none

This song is a fun way to celebrate Jesus' birth. Sing these words to the tune of "Ten Little Indians." Then add the motions, and proclaim Jesus' birth together.

Let's Play

One little, two little, three little wise men *(hold up one, then two, then three fingers)*

Followed a star all the way to Bethlehem, *(march in place and point to sky)*

Found baby Jesus, and gave him presents. *(Bow and pretend to hand out presents.)*

"Glo-ry to God!" *(Raise arms toward heaven.)*

Praise Parade

Supplies: "Praise Parade" handout (p. 112)

This song is a great way to act out Psalm 150.

Let's Play

Cut apart the slips from the "Praise Parade" handout and put them in a box. You'll need one slip for each child in your class.

Have the children stand in a circle. Have one child draw out a slip. Have the children march in the circle while pretending to play the instruments illustrated on the slips. They can make noises to go with their instruments, such as "Boom! Boom!" for the drums or "Clang! Clang!" for cymbals.

You may want the children to pretend to play specific songs such as "Twinkle, Twinkle, Little Star," "Jesus Loves Me," or "Praise Him (All You Little Children)."

Continue until each instrument has been played. For extra fun, let children draw slips together to create a band!

Candle Counting

Supplies: none

Sing this song during the days before Christmas, or use it any time you want to sing about Jesus.

Let's Play

Have the children hold up their fingers to represent candles as they sing the countdown to Christmas. Children can "blow out" a candle as they sing each verse. Continue singing each of these verses to the tune of the first half of "Twinkle, Twinkle, Little Star."

Ten little candles for Jesus shine.
Whh! Whh! Whh! Now there are nine! *(Put one finger down.)*

Nine little candles, the whole world waits.
Whh! Whh! Whh! Now there are eight! *(Put one finger down.)*

Praise Parade

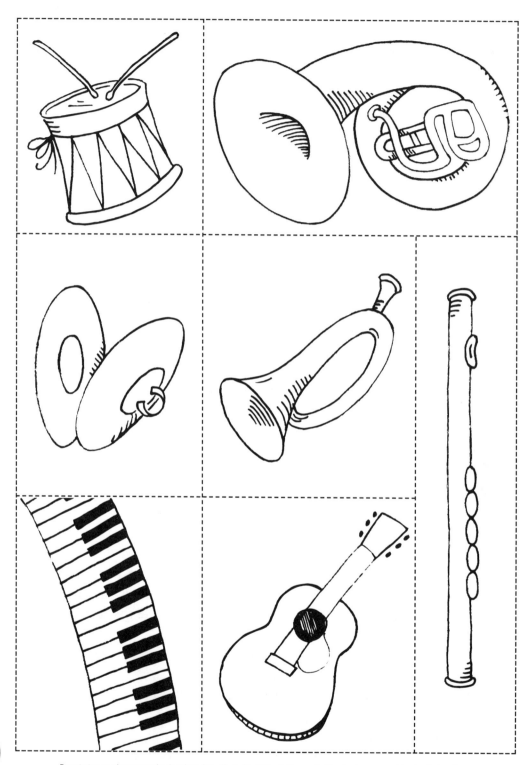

Eight little candles, a star from heaven.
Whh! Whh! Whh! Now there are seven. *(Put one finger down.)*

Seven little candles, follow—quick!
Whh! Whh! Whh! Now there are six. *(Put one finger down.)*

Six little candles, shepherds arrive.
Whh! Whh! Whh! Now there are five. *(Put one finger down.)*

Five little candles, a manger poor.
Whh! Whh! Whh! Now there are four. *(Put one finger down.)*

Four little candles, can it be?
Whh! Whh! Whh! Now there are three. *(Put one finger down.)*

Three little candles, a promise true.
Whh! Whh! Whh! Now there are two. *(Put one finger down.)*

Two little candles, wise men come.
Whh! Whh! Whh! Now there is one. *(Put one finger down.)*

One little candle, God's own son.
He brought love for everyone. *(Hold one finger up high.)*

For extra fun, let each child hold an unlit birthday candle, or make construction paper candles to hold.

Shipwreck

Supplies: none

Use this song about Paul's shipwreck (Acts 27:13-44) to teach that God protects us even when we have troubles.

Let's Play

Choose one child to be "Paul" and two children to be "sailors." Have everyone else form the "boat" by joining hands in a circle around Paul

113

and the sailors.

Then sing this song to the tune of "This Old Man." Sing it once, then add the motions:

The boat went up. (*Have children who formed the boat stand on their tiptoes.*)

The boat went down. (*Have the boat crouch down on the floor.*)

The sailors tumbled all around. (*Have sailors and Paul move back and forth inside the boat.*)

When the boat began to sink, they thought they were done. (*Have the boat lie down on the floor. Have Paul and the sailors cover their heads.*)

But God protected everyone! (*Have everyone fold his or her hands in prayer.*)

►Clap Your Hands

Supplies: none

This is a fun and simple praise song that children can add their own verses to.

Let's Play

Sing this song to the tune of "Clementine."

Clap your hands; clap your hands;
Clap your hands and praise the Lord.
Clap your hands; clap your hands;
Clap your hands, and praise the Lord.

Use these motions to create other verses for the song.
● jump up high
● bend down low
● turn around
● hop on one foot
● shake your body
● nod your head
● wiggle everything

To challenge older preschoolers, combine two actions. For example, sing, "Clap your hands; stamp your feet. Do all this to praise the Lord."

Heavenly Helpers

Supplies: none

Use the following rhyme when you teach Psalm 91:11: "He has put his angels in charge of you to watch over you wherever you go."

Let's Play

God sends angels from above (point to heaven),
To keep us safe, to show his love. *(Fold hands over heart.)*
An angel on the left *(tap your left shoulder)*
And an angel on the right *(tap your right shoulder),*
God keeps us safe all through the night. *(Close eyes and snore.)*
The bright sun comes to wake the day. *(Rub eyes and stretch arms overhead.)*
Then angels watch us as we play. *(Wave.)*

Ten to One

Supplies: none

Use this song when your lesson is about the one man who returned to thank Jesus for healing him (Luke 17:11-19).

Let's Play

Have the children hold both hands in front of them with fingers pointing up to begin this fun finger play.

115

Ten lepers came to Jesus one day. *(Wiggle all 10 fingers.)*

"Please make us well," he heard them say. *(Fold hands in prayer.)*
He said what to do, and they all obeyed. *(Point with pointer finger.)*
So Jesus healed them right away. *(Clap on each syllable of "right away.")*
Excited and happy they ran awhile. *(Make hands jump up and down,
then wiggle fingers in a running motion.)*
But one came back with a thankful smile *(hold up one finger)*.

Do You Know Who Jesus Is?

Supplies: masking tape

This song is a fun variation of a cakewalk.

Let's Play

Have the children stand in a circle. Put a masking tape X on the floor.
Have the children hold hands and walk in a circle as you all sing this
song to the tune of "The Muffin Man."

Oh, do you know who Jesus is,
Who Jesus is, who Jesus is?
Oh, do you know who Jesus is?
He is the Son of God.

Stand in the middle of the circle, and sing the next verse while the
children switch directions and continue walking.

Oh, yes, I know who Jesus is,
Who Jesus is, who Jesus is.
Oh, yes, I know who Jesus is,
He is the Son of God.

At the end of this verse, have whoever is standing on the X join you
in the middle of the circle. Let the rest of the children change directions
and sing this verse.

Now two of us know who Jesus is,
Who Jesus is, who Jesus is.
Now two of us know who Jesus is,
He is the Son of God.

Again, at the end of the verse, have the child standing on the X join those in the middle of the circle. Have the group change directions again, and continue walking while singing, "Now three of us know who Jesus is..."

Continue until the entire class is in the middle. To end the game, lead the class in singing, "Now we all know who Jesus is..."

Jesus Calms the Storm

Supplies: none

Use this song during a lesson about how Jesus calmed the storm. (Mark 4:35-41).

Let's Play

Sing this song to the tune of "Row, Row, Row Your Boat." Then teach the children the motions and let them sing and act out the story.

Row, row, row your boat *(row with both hands)*
On the stormy sea. *(Sway back and forth.)*
The wind is blowing very hard. *(Sway and wave arms in the air.)*
And waves wash over me. *(Hide under arms.)*

Jesus stands up very tall *(stand up)*
And calls out, "Peace. Be still!" *(Put finger over lips.)*
The wind and waves obey his voice. *(Extend hand in a stop motion.)*
The storm obeys his will. *(Fall to ground.)*

Head to Toe

Supplies: none

Preschoolers are proud of their ability to identify the different parts of their bodies.

Let's Play

Sing this song to the tune of "Skip to My Lou," and have the children point to each body part as it's mentioned.

God made my body, head to toe.
God made my body, head to toe.
God made my body, head to toe.
My body, head to toe.

Verse 2: God made every hair on my head.
Verse 3: God made my eyes, my mouth, and my nose.
Verse 4: God made my shoulders and my neck.
Verse 5: God made my elbows and my hands.
Verse 6: God made my fingers, 10 of them.
Verse 7: God made my stomach and my back.
Verse 8: God made my heart and even my skin.
Verse 9: God made my legs, my knees, and my toes.

This Little Light of Mine

Supplies: none

Form pairs to sing this favorite song.

Let's Play

This little light of mine, *(Hold "light" overhead.)*
I'm gonna let it shine.
This little light of mine,
I'm gonna let it shine.
Let it shine, let it shine, let it shine.

Hide it under a bushel? No! *(Crouch down, and pop up on the word "no.")*
I'm gonna let it shine.
Hide it under a bushel? No!
I'm gonna let it shine.
Let it shine, let it shine, let it shine.

Shine all over (name of your town). *(Wave arm in an overhead circle.)*
I'm gonna let it shine.
Shine all over (name of your town).
I'm gonna let it shine.
Let it shine, let it shine, let it shine.

Mighty David

Supplies: none

Teach the children this simple finger play that tells the story of David and Goliath (1 Samuel 17:1-58).

Let's Play

Goliath was a giant tall *(reach up high)*
With arms as thick as trees! *(Hold your arms as if hugging a big tree.)*
He'd laugh and say, "I can do it all! *(Pat chest.)*
There's nobody bigger than me!" *(Flex muscles.)*

David was a shepherd small *(hold hand down low)*,
Not very big, you see. *(Show empty hands.)*

He walked right up and began to call *(make megaphone with hands)*,
"Today God will be with me!" *(Cross arms over chest.)*

David took a little stone *(gather stone from the ground)*
And put it in his sling. *(Place rock in imaginary sling.)*
He ran out to battle all alone *(make running motion with fingers)*
To see what God would bring. *(Point toward heaven.)*

He twirled the stone 'round and 'round *(twirl hand over head)*
Then slung with all his might. *(Twirl hand over head.)*
Goliath fell upon the ground. *(Tap forehead.)*
Young David won the fight! *(Raise arms in victory.)*

Have the class say this cheer to end the rhyme: "Yea! Yea! God saved the day!"

The Ladder Song

Supplies: none

This is an easy song to learn for Christmastime.

Let's Play

Sing this song using the eight successive tones in the scale. Start the first verse at the high end of the scale and sing down. Have the children move their hands or their bodies from high in the air to low near the ground. Then start the second verse at the low end of the scale and sing up. Have the children move their hands or their bodies from down near the ground to high in the air.

Little baby
Jesus
Came down to
Earth on the
Bright morning

Of the first
Christmas
Day.

I will sing
Glad praises
Because of
Jesus' birth.
And I'll send my
Praises
Up to
God.

Praises!

Supplies: none

Teach your children that singing is a way of praising God.

Let's Play

Sing this song to the tune of "Camptown Races" and lead your class in the accompanying motions for lots of fun.

Happy Christians sing to God. *(Clap to the beat.)*
Praises! Praises! *(Jump and wave hands on each word.)*
Happy Christians sing to God, praises all day long. *(Clap to the beat.)*

When I rise and shine *(wiggle fingers by face to look like sun rays)*,
'Til I go to bed *(cradle face on hands)*,
Happy Christians sing to God, praises all day long. *(Clap to the beat.)*

Older preschoolers will enjoy adding times when they praise God, such as "When I eat my lunch, 'til I play outside."

Stand Up, Sit Down

Supplies: none

Older preschoolers will enjoy taking turns leading the class in this game.

Let's Play

Sing a familiar song to the children, such as "Jesus Loves Me." Sing some of the words very loudly. Sing other words very softly. Have the children stand for the loud words and sit for the soft words.

During the second verse, gradually sing more loudly as the children rise from a sitting position to a standing position. Then gradually sing softly as the children slowly sink back down to a sitting position.

Thankfulness

Supplies: masking tape

Children will have a chance to thank God for specific things during this song.

Let's Play

Have the children stand in a circle. Put a masking tape X on the floor.

Sing this song to the tune of "Polly Wolly Doodle," and lead the children in the actions. Have the children walk in a circle while singing the first four lines. Then have them stop and clap while singing the fifth line. At the end of the song, have whoever's standing on the X mention two things to be thankful for. It's OK if children repeat some of the same things, such as families and homes.

My God gives me so many things *(walk in a circle)*;
I'll thank him every day.
For the food I eat

And the clothes I wear,
I'll say, "Thank you, thank you, all day!" *(Stop and clap to the beat.)*

Sit down *(squat down)*,
Stand up *(stand up)*,
Then turn a circle 'round. *(Turn around in a circle.)*
For the many things
God gives to me,
I'll say, "Thank you, thank you, all day!" *(Clap to the beat.)*

Continue walking and singing until all of the children have suggested ideas.

►Hooray! Hooray!

Supplies: none

This song uses unique motions. Be prepared for giggles!

Let's Play

Have the children sit in a tight circle with their legs extended in front of them. Sing this song to the tune of "When Johnny Comes Marching Home."

God gave me feet to walk and run. *(Wave feet back and forth to the beat.)*
Hooray! *(Lift up right foot.)*
Hooray! *(Lift up left foot.)*
God gave me feet to walk and run. *(Wave feet back and forth to the beat.)*
Hooray! *(Lift up right foot.)*
Hooray! *(Lift up left foot.)*

I'll march along *(bend right knee and put foot flat)*
And sing this song. *(Bend left knee and put foot flat.)*
I'll tell of God's love *(straighten right leg)*

All day long. *(Straighten left leg.)*

And my feet will help me *(wave your feet back and forth to the beat)*
To serve the Lord each day. *(Wave your feet back and forth to the beat.)*

River Reeds

Supplies: small basket

This is a great song to sing when your lesson is about baby Moses (Exodus 2:1-11).

Let's Play

Have the children stand in a circle and pretend to be river reeds. Encourage them to raise their arms. Choose one child to be "It." Have It stand in the middle of the circle and close his or her eyes while the rest of the children sing this song to the tune of "A-Tiskit, A-Tasket."

A-tiskit, A-taskit. Put Moses in a basket.
Set it in the river reeds.
God will take care of his needs.

Give the children a tiny basket to pass around. At the end of the song, have the child with the basket hide it behind his or her back. Have all of the other children hide their hands too. Have It guess who has the basket. If It guesses correctly, he or she trades places with the child who has the basket. If It doesn't guess correctly in two tries, he or she is It for another round. Continue the song until everyone has had a chance to be It.

Peter's Escape

Supplies: none

Bring Peter's story (Acts 12:1-17) to life with this action rhyme.

Let's Play

Have the children sit in a circle and follow your actions.

Peter talked about God's love. *(Open and close hands.)*
And that made some folks mad. *(Put hands on hips.)*
They carried Peter off to jail. *(Lift hands in a carrying motion.)*
His friends from church were sad. *(Hug self and look sad.)*

With chains upon his hands and feet *(touch hands and feet)*,
Poor Peter fell asleep. *(Cradle face on hands.)*
His friends back home prayed all night long *(pretend to yawn)*
They prayed; they didn't weep! *(Fold hands in prayer.)*

Soon a light shone all around. *(Spread hands around face.)*
The cell was bright as day! *(Shield eyes.)*
The chains on Peter's hands and feet *(cross wrists)*
Quickly fell away. *(Uncross hands and hold them wide open.)*

God's angel lead him out of jail. *(Point in several directions.)*
He told him, "Follow me." *(Wave "come here.")*
Then Peter walked to Mary's house *(make hands walk)*
And knocked there, one, two, three. *(Knock on floor three times.)*

The praying people were surprised. *(Put hands on cheeks.)*
"Peter's here—come see!" *(Shield eyes with hands.)*
And Peter told them all, with joy *(draw smile on face)*,
That God had set him free! *(Point to heaven.)*

125

Ruth and Naomi

Supplies: none

Have fun with this finger play about Ruth and Naomi (Ruth 2).

Let's Play

Have the children sit in a circle and follow your motions.

Ruth and Naomi were two good chums *(wiggle both thumbs)*,
Who needed food for their empty tums. *(Rub tummy.)*
Naomi made bread. *(Wiggle one thumb.)*
Ruth gathered wheat. *(Wiggle the other thumb.)*
Then they thanked God for the treat. *(Fold hands in prayer.)*
Yummy good bread. *(Rub tummy with one hand.)*
Yummy good bread. *(Rub tummy with the other hand.)*
Thank you, God, for this yummy good bread. *(Rub tummy with both hands.)*

For fun, have the children gather scattered popcorn kernels after this rhyme, then serve them popped popcorn as a treat.

Four Read-Along Stories That Unfold Before Your Children's Eyes!

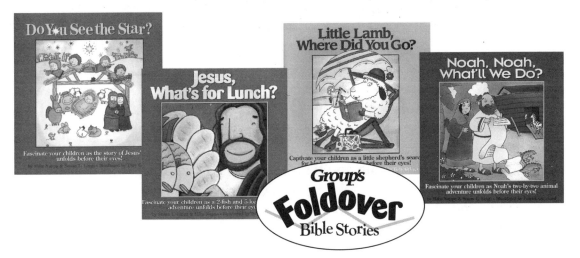

Treat your children to books that take storytelling to *new lengths*— a full 80 inches!

Each **Foldover Bible Story** invites your children to help solve a problem...

- *Do You See The Star?* follows a shepherd as he searches for a distant glow.
  ISBN 1-55945-617-5

- *Jesus, What's for Lunch?* considers a favorite Bible story from the viewpoint of child who is way past lunch time.
  ISBN 1-55945-620-5

- In *Little Lamb, Where Did You Go?* children join a young shepherd in looking high and low for a lost lamb.
  ISBN 1-55945-618-3

- In *Noah, Noah, What'll We Do?* Noah needs help sorting out mixed-up animals.
  ISBN 1-55945-619-1

Lively, rhyming text and vivid illustrations hint at possible solutions, so even your youngest children will offer suggestions as the story unfolds. But not until the very last panel is everything clear!

Bonus "For Extra Fun" pages give you new craft and snack ideas to explore and to help you celebrate these stories with your children!

Order all four **Foldover Bible Story** books *now* and delight children in Sunday school...children's church...preschool...at home...*anywhere* children love to snuggle up to a good story!

Order today from your local Christian bookstore, or write: Group Publishing, Box 485, Loveland, CO 80539.

TEACH YOUR PRESCHOOLERS AS JESUS TAUGHT WITH GROUP'S *HANDS-ON BIBLE CURRICULUM*™

Hands-On Bible Curriculum™ for preschoolers helps your preschoolers learn the way they learn best—by touching, exploring, and discovering. With active learning, preschoolers love learning about the Bible, and they really remember what they learn.

Because small children learn best through repetition, Preschoolers and Pre-K & K will learn one important point per lesson, and Toddlers & 2s will learn one point each month with **Hands-On Bible Curriculum**. These important lessons will stick with them and comfort them during their daily lives. Your children will learn:

- •God is our friend,
- •who Jesus is, and
- •we can always trust Jesus.

The **Learning Lab®** is packed with age-appropriate learning tools for fun, faith-building lessons. Toddlers & 2s explore big **Interactive StoryBoards**™ with enticing textures that toddlers love to touch. **Bible Big Books**™ captivate Preschoolers and Pre-K & K while teaching them important Bible lessons. With **Jumbo Bible Puzzles**™ and involving **Learning Mats**™, your children will see, touch, and explore their Bible stories. Each quarter there's a brand new collection of supplies to keep your lessons fresh and involving.

Fuzzy, age-appropriate hand puppets are also available to add to the learning experience. These child-friendly puppets help you teach each lesson with scripts provided in the **Teachers Guide**. Cuddles the Lamb, Whiskers the Mouse, and Pockets the Kangaroo turn each lesson into an interactive and entertaining learning experience.

Just order one **Learning Lab** and one **Teachers Guide** for each age level, add a few common classroom supplies, and presto—you have everything you need to build faith in your children. For more interactive fun, introduce your children to the age-appropriate puppet who will be your teaching assistant and their friend. **No student books required!**

Hands-On Bible Curriculum is also available for grades 1–6.